Asahigawa

Otaru
Sapporo
HOKKAIDO

Noboribetsu

Kushiro

Hakodate

Aomori

Akita

Morioka

SADO
ISLAND

Yamagata
Matsushima
Niigata
Sendai

Fukushima

Nagano

Nikko

Maebashi
Utsunomiya

Kofu
Mito

Urawa
*ji*▲
TOKYO
akone
Yokohama
Chiba
tami
Kamakura
Ito

N

# JAPAN

0        100        200miles

0      100      200      300km

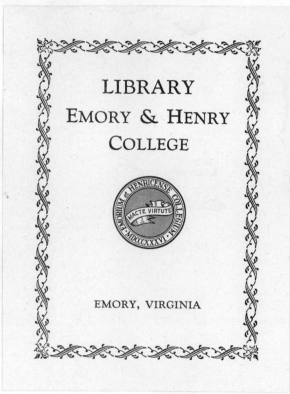

# JAPAN

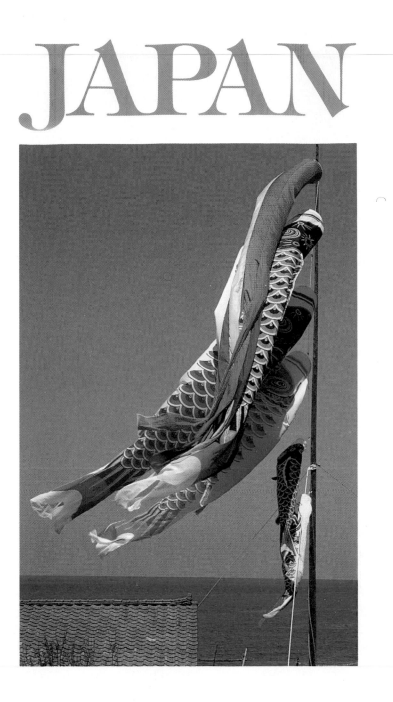

# JAPAN

## PETER SPRY-LEVERTON & PETER KORNICKI
### Photographs by Joel Sackett

**Facts On File Publications**
New York, New York ● Oxford, England

First published in the United States by Facts on File Inc., 1988
460 Park Avenue South
New York   NY10016

By arrangement with Michael O'Mara Books
20 Queen Anne Street
London W1N 9FB

**Library of Congress Cataloging-in-Publication Data**
Spry-Leverton, Peter.
  Japan.
  Bibliography: p.
  Includes index.
  1. Japan—History—20th century.   2. Japan—Social life and customs—20th
century.   I. Kornicki, Peter F. (Peter Francis)   II. Title.
DS885.S68   1988        952.03'3          87-13656
ISBN 0-8160-1845-6

# For Lisa and Catharine

Printed in Spain

10 9 8 7 6 5 4 3 2 1

Illustrations on
Page 1: Huge carp streamers made of paper or cloth are flown on Boys' Day, an annual festival
held on 5 May. The carp symbolizes courage and ambition.

Pages 2-3: A spectacular outside performance by a drummer of the world-famous Kodo
Ensemble

# Contents

# Acknowledgments

**Authors' Acknowledgments**

This book was written at the same time as the television series was being planned, shot and edited. During that process many hundreds of people went out of their way to help and guide the making of the series. The crew is listed separately and to them I express my grateful thanks for all their hard work and creative insight.

I would also like to thank: Richard Creasey, Philip Jones and Roger James of Central TV; Paul Bonner, Carol Haslam and John Ranelagh of Channel Four; Pat Faust and Bruce Mundt of WTTW; Sue Henny of the Japan Foundation in London; in the United States Rand Castile, Peter Grilli and Carol Gluck; Lawrence Smith; Joe Earle; Michiko Ikeda; Leslie Downer; The Kodo Drummers of Sado Island; John Kaizan Neptune; Thomas E. McLain; Chizuko Kobayashi and Motoo Sakurai of NHK; Zensho Ota; Katsumobu Takechi; Shinsaku Sogo; Kamo Harada; Kim Schufftan; Professor Yoshihiro Misono; Joel Sackett; Ian Baruma; Otto Fried; Issey Miyake; Mr Hayashi; and finally, Lisa, Edward and Anna.

Peter Spry-Leverton

I wish to thank my father, Squadron Leader Franciszek Kornicki, and my father-in-law, Dr Samuel J. Mikolaski, for the collections of newspaper cuttings relating to Japan which they have built up for me over the years and which proved invaluable when writing this book.

Peter Kornicki

**Production Credits**

|  |  |
|---|---|
| *Producer/Director* | Peter Spry-Leverton |
| *Camera* | Peter Greenhalgh |
|  | Grahame Wickings |
| *Additional Photography* | Chris Fryman |
| *Sound Recordist* | Bill Dodkin |
| *Interpreter* | Yukiko Shimahara |
| *Graphics* | Frameline |
| *Research* | Alastair Laurence |
| *Production Assistant* | Julie Stoner |
| *Film Editor* | Jonathan Morris |
| *Assistant Editor* | Tony Pound |

**Illustration Acknowledgments**

The photographer, Joel Sackett, would like to thank Olympus Photo Plaza staff in Tokyo for the generous technical support extended to him during the course of his work on this book. Most of the photographs were shot using OM-1 and OM-4 cameras, and a range of lenses from 24 mm to 180 mm. In addition the Leica range-finder was used in low-lit situations.

The authors and publisher would like to thank the following for permission to reproduce illustrations in the book:

By permission of the Syndics of Cambridge University Library: 61 (from *Moko shurai ekotoba*); 63 (from *Kitabatake monogatari*); 69 (from *Nisshin senso emaki*); 127 (from *Owari meisho zue*); 129 (from *Musashi abumi*); 131 (from *Ansei kenmonshi*); Robert Hunt Library: 75, 77, 79, 81; Peter Kornicki: 94, 96; *News Chronicle*/British Library: 23; Spencer Collection, New York Public Library (Photo: Robert Rubic/Precision Chromes Inc, New York): 90 (from Japanese Ms 53); Toa Trading Co. Ltd, Nagoya: 13, 14, 46, 57, 59, 101, 104, 130, 152

The endpaper map was drawn by Eugene Fleury

**General Acknowledgments**

The authors and publisher would like to thank the following for permission to reprint extracts within this book. Details of the extracts are listed under the Bibliographical References on page 188.

Allen & Unwin (Publishers) Ltd; The Athlone Press; Australian Government Publishing Service; Columbia University Press; Dow Jones & Company and *The Wall Street Journal*; Faber & Faber Ltd; *Far Eastern Economic Review*; *Financial Times*; *The Guardian*; *The Listener*; *The Literary Review*; New Directions Publishing Corporation and UNESCO; *New Scientist*; Secker & Warburg; The University of California Press; UNESCO and the University of Tokyo Press; Weatherhill

We apologize if there are copyright holders who have not been acknowledged but assure them that every effort has been made to contact them. On application to the publisher they will receive any reasonable fee that may be due.

# Chronology

Here and throughout this book Japanese names are given in the Japanese order, with surname followed by given name.

710-794    NARA PERIOD. Nara is the capital for most of this period, which marks the highwater-mark of Chinese influence on Japan.

794-1185    HEIAN PERIOD. In 794 the capital is established at Kyoto, which was at the time called 'Heian-kyo'; it remained the capital until 1868.

1185-1333    KAMAKURA PERIOD. Government passes into the hands of the samurai class, headed by a hereditary line of shoguns who establish their headquarters at Kamakura, near contemporary Tokyo.

1333-1600    MUROMACHI PERIOD. A new line of shoguns takes over, governing from the Muromachi quarter of Kyoto. In the 15th and 16th centuries much of Japan is racked by civil war, but successive attempts to reunify Japan are made by Oda Nobunaga, Toyotomi Hideyoshi and Tokugawa Ieyasu.

1600-1868    TOKUGAWA PERIOD. After the battle of Sekigahara in 1600, Tokugawa Ieyasu establishes a new line of shoguns in Edo. The succeeding centuries are a period of economic and urban growth but in the 19th century the deteriorating economy and the growing threat from Europe and America lead to the collapse of the shogunate and to the Meiji Restoration.

1868-1912    MEIJI PERIOD.

1868    The Meiji Restoration brings about a nominal restoration of power to the Emperor Meiji and ushers in a period of intense Westernization.

1889    The promulgation of the Constitution.

1894-5    The Sino-Japanese War.

1904-5    The Russo-Japanese War.

1910    Japan annexes Korea.

1912-1926    TAISHO PERIOD. Coincides with the reign of Emperor Taisho, who was mentally unstable and little more than a figurehead.

1914    Japan declares war on Germany and acquires German possessions in the Far East.

1925    Universal suffrage for men.

1926-    SHOWA PERIOD. The period begins with the accession of the present Emperor, whose given name, Hirohito, is rarely used in Japan. 'Showa' is the name given to his reign.

1937    War with China breaks out. In December thousands of civilians are massacred in the Rape of Nanking.

1941    The attack on Pearl Harbor and the sinking of two British battleships initiate the Pacific War.

1945    Atomic bombs dropped on Hiroshima and Nagasaki precipitate Japan's surrender.

1946    A New Constitution is promulgated establishing the foundations of a parliamentary democracy and extending the franchise to women.

1952    Following the treaty of San Francisco, the Occupation comes to an end and Japan resumes her independent status.

1955    Liberal-Democratic Party formed. It has now maintained its majority in parliament for more than 30 years.

## CHAPTER ONE

# Through Western Eyes

A few years ago a Japanese professor lecturing in France was surprised to hear himself being referred to as a 'messenger from the black hole'. Puzzled, he sought out his host afterwards and asked for an explanation. The answer was that modern Japan is for most Westerners a black hole in space, from which no clear picture or information ever escapes. Few people have learned anything about Japan in school or at university, and fewer still have any first-hand experience to rely on. Small wonder, then, that much of the information about Japan that reaches us relies heavily on stereotyped but reassuringly familiar images, like the bespectacled businessman, the ferocious samurai bristling with sharp steel, or the willowy geisha.

The cartoon Japanese businessman is a good example. His buck teeth pour out of a gaping mouth, his eyes are slanted and narrow enough for a single stroke of the pen, he is small and chubby, and his goggle-eye glasses are out-of-date enough to be antique. We can recognize him for what he is supposed to be, but he seems today even less realistic than the cartoon Frenchman, with his beret, his gauloise and loaves under his arm. It goes without saying that the cartoon businessman is almost as hard to find in Japan today as sword-waving samurai and would-be kamikaze pilots, though they too continue to feature as stock cartoon figures. Much the same goes for the more contemporary images of Japan as a concrete jungle teeming with besuited workaholics on their way to or from their rabbit-hutch homes. There may be grains of truth in such images, but they are still misleading and not conducive to understanding.

The main religions in Japan are Buddhism and Shinto but several others, including Christianity, coexist with them. (Left) A Christian nun squats beside a pool of ornamental carp. The Jesuit missionaries in the sixteenth century did much to spread the Christian word. On the right a Buddhist nun, with shaved head, walks beside the castle walls at Himeji.

The Catholic church on Amakusa island off the west coast of Kyushu. There are few Christians in Japan today, about a million, but there are many churches dating from the heyday of missionary activity in the late nineteenth century.

Whatever may be true in the past or the future, Japan is at the present a country of great moment in the economic affairs of the world and increasingly too in its political affairs. As such, it is clearly a country that other nations remain ignorant of at their peril. So, however convenient and even amusing the stereotypes may be, they need replacing. In a similar way, some early Japanese images of Europe and America needed replacing in the late nineteenth century. Knowledge of the outside world had been hard to come by in Japan until the 1850s, when pressure from America and Russia forced an end to more than two centuries of seclusion. Once the wall had

been breeched a trickle of information, later to become a flood, began to flow into Japan. At first this information was unsystematic and disconnected and in such circumstances ignorance was prey to all that imagination can provide. This became all too clear when misinformation and grotesque rumours began to circulate along with the news and knowledge. As the new-fangled telegraph lines, for example, began to reach across the country, a rumour went around to the effect that the lines would only work if they had been smeared with the blood of virgins. From this it was easy to conclude that the object of the national census was really to find out just how many such virgins were available for this purpose.

The Japan that Marco Polo heard about during his long stay in China in the thirteenth century was a country awash with gold, but it was not until the middle of the sixteenth century that Europeans first set foot in Japan to discover that this was far from true. These first Europeans on Japanese soil were Portuguese, at the furthest extremities of their seaborne empire. Over the course of the next hundred years they were to be followed by Spaniards, English, Dutch and even by Poles, who travelled to Japan to trade or to spread Christianity. They are of interest to us here because of the letters and reports they sent home and the perceptions of Japan that emerge from these various sources. For some of these letters and reports were published, a few in the course of the sixteenth century, and they constituted the only first-hand knowledge of Japan and its people available to Western eyes in Europe at that time.

*Right* Sunset over the Japan Sea. Japan is made up of four main islands: Hokkaido in the north, Honshu, the main island, Shikoku the smallest, and Kyushu the southernmost. There are some 4,000 smaller islands but the fifth largest is Sado Island where a number of the photographs in this book were taken.

*Left* Stalls beside a busy road provide late-night snacks for people returning home.

Most of these early visitors shared one prejudice, albeit one that at the time was an article of faith. For both the missionaries and the other writers it was inescapable that the Japanese were pagans, their Buddhist images mere idols, their gods nothing more than devils, and their devotions false and mistaken. This matter apart, however, the Jesuit missionaries and the traders proved to be perceptive and even sympathetic observers of Japan in the sixteenth and seventeenth centuries, and also to be surprisingly free of prejudices.

One of the most enthusiastic missionaries in Japan during the sixteenth century was St Francis Xavier, who regarded the Japanese language, with some reason, as a language invented by the devil to frustrate the work of missionaries in Japan. Although mindful that the Japanese were after all pagans, he formed a very favourable impression of their qualities, as the following extract shows:

*Below* A nineteenth-century photograph showing rickshawmen waiting for business on a city street. The rickshaw dates from the 1870s.

Judging by the people we have so far met, I would say that the Japanese are the best race yet discovered and I do not think you will find their match among the pagan nations. They are very sociable, usually good and not malicious, and much concerned with their honour, which they prize above everything else.

The face of the old cities changed in the nineteenth century as the influence of the West began to reach Japan. Western-style buildings and gas lamps began to appear in the streets.

An equally good impression of Japanese children appears in the writings of François Caron, who reached Japan in the early years of the seventeenth century and remained there until 1639 in the service of the Dutch East India Company:

> It is remarkable to see how orderly and how modestly little children of seven or eight years old behave themselves; their discourse and answers savouring of riper age, and far surpassing any I have yet seen of their times in our country.

John Saris, a Yorkshireman who arrived in Japan in 1613 and stayed for six months, left this description of an execution and his admiration for the bearing of the condemned man is undisguised:

> I saw one led to execution who went so resolutely and without all appearance of fear of death that I could not but much admire him, never having seen the like in Christendom. The offence for which he suffered was for stealing of a sack of rice from his neighbour, whose house was then on fire.

Urban life in Japan also impressed these early European observers, among them the Portuguese Jesuit known as Rodrigues the Interpreter, who sailed to Japan at the age of 15. He became so proficient at Japanese that he served as interpreter for both Hideyoshi and Ieyasu, successive *de facto* rulers of Japan, and wrote several works on Japanese language and history. He was finally expelled in 1610, after more than 30 years in Japan. Writing an account of what he called 'the noble and populous city of Miyako', the city now known as Kyoto, he had this to say:

> The city is extremely clean and in each of its broad streets is to be found water from excellent springs and streams which run along the middle. The streets are swept and sprinkled with water twice a day and are thus kept very clean and fresh, for every man looks after the part in front of his own house.

Rodrigues also developed a taste for Japanese art and summed up its characteristics with remarkable perception and understanding:

> Although they copy nature in their paintings, they do not like a multitude and crowd of things in pictures, but prefer to portray, even in a sumptuous and lovely place, just a few solitary things with due proportion between them, and indeed they distinguish themselves in this respect. But they know very little about painting the human body and its various parts and they can hardly be compared with our painters as regards the portrayal of the body itself and the proportions of its members.

It is clear from these quotations that the Europeans in Japan in the sixteenth and seventeenth centuries did not bring with them so overwhelming a sense of their own superiority that they were unable to make fair and sometimes favourable judgments about all they observed during their time in Japan. They had unfavourable judgments to make too, and they found a good deal of vice to censure, as the following passage from the writings of the Jesuit Valignano shows. He had three spells of residence in Japan at the end of the sixteenth century and praised the Japanese as loudly for their virtues of prudence and bravery as he condemned them for their moral shortcomings.

> Their first bad quality is that they are much addicted to sensual vices and sins, a thing which has always been true of pagans. The men do not pay much attention to what their wives do in this respect because they trust them exceedingly, but both husbands and relatives may kill an adulterous wife and her partner at will. But even worse is their great dissipation in the sin that does not bear mentioning. This is regarded so lightly that both the boys and the men who consort with them brag and talk about it openly without trying to cover the matter up.

Cruelty was the other subject that caught the attention of these Western visitors. English visitors such as John Saris and Richard Cocks, as well as the Jesuits, wrote with disgust of the sight of corpses by the roadside, left after execution as a warning to others, of minor offenders crucified and left to hang on their crosses after death, of families punished for the crimes of a single member, and of the custom of testing sword-blades on the corpses of criminals. The harshness of law and penalty in Japan became particularly poignant topics when the favours extended to the missionaries came to an end in the seventeenth century and the persecution of both missionary and convert began.

Mr Hamada, a master of folk puppetry, performs on Sado Island. The National Theatres in Tokyo and Osaka offer productions of *bunraku* which are internationally celebrated but owe their roots in part to rural folk puppetry.

A century of intercourse between Europe and Japan came to a gory end, though the body of knowledge that had by this time been accumulated in Europe was in many respects balanced and accurate. With a few exceptions, it was not until the 1850s and 1860s that significant numbers of Europeans were to set foot on Japanese soil again. By then, of course, Europe had passed through a period of momentous change during the Industrial Revolution and as a result the technological gap between Japan and Europe was much wider than it had been in the early seventeenth century. Indeed, the gap was so wide that some doubted whether it could be bridged at all.

Who were these nineteenth-century visitors to Japan? In addition to Europeans there were now Americans as well. There were, of course, missionaries again, but this time the Catholic missions were overshadowed by those of the Protestants. They came prepared not only to preach but also to educate, nurse, campaign against prostitution and drunkenness, and to care for orphans and to engage in other forms of pastoral work. There were also the globe-trotters: the development of the new steamship routes between Japan and California made it possible to circumnavigate the globe and to do so in some comfort. There were the paid employees of the new Meiji government, hired to facilitate the rapid industrialization and Westernization of Japan: they ranged from teachers of English, scientists and legal advisers to navvies and lighthousemen. There was also the usual transient population of port towns, the 'ne'er-do-wells' with impossible dreams of striking it rich, like the American who was the first to hit upon the idea of importing claret to Japan, and then the first to discover that the Japanese did not drink it.

Many of these nineteenth-century visitors and residents put their impressions to paper as well, in letters and also in numerous books and magazine articles. So much did they write that it is difficult to generalize, but it is fair to say that a feeling of inherent Western superiority is often to be detected near the surface; this time there was more readiness to be critical, condescending or even contemptuous. Whereas Valignano had expressed his admiration for some of the characteristics of Japanese art, an English journalist writing 250 years later had nothing but contempt for it.

> English art is always said by its practitioners to be in a parlous way, but at its worst it has not been anything like so cheap, so feeble, and so squalid as is the best art of Japan. . . . Hundreds of men have spent thousands of pounds on Japanese stuff when the craze was on them, and been glad to get rid of it for an old song when their sanity came back to them.

In these European writings there was also a sense of puzzlement. Kipling expressed this most clearly when he wrote in 1900: 'The Chinaman's a native . . . but the Jap isn't a native, and he isn't a sahib either.' The view that Kipling is expressing here, one of seeing the Japanese as a superior sort of native, was quite widespread and it usually came to the fore in comparisons of Japan with China. Such comparisons were common, if only because the usual itineraries along the steamship routes invariably took travellers to some port in China either on the way out or returning home. The concensus was that China was less civilized, as is apparent from the following passage that appeared in *The Times* in 1876:

> Japanese cleanliness as opposed to Chinese filth; Japanese roads as opposed to Chinese mud tracks; Japanese neatness and order as opposed to Chinese decay and confusion . . . If there is a yard of spare ground alongside a cottage in Japan, there will be a tiny shrub or two, a few tastefully arranged pebbles, and probably a little fountain; in China there would be a rubbish heap.

If the Japanese were seen to be superior to the Chinese by European and American travellers, this by no means meant that it was thought they were

*Above* Along an unspoiled coastline seaweed is drying in the sun. Seaweed is used in the kitchen to make stocks and pickles and as an accompaniment to various dishes such as *tempura* in which fish, vegetables and seaweed are cooked in batter.

capable of catching up with the West. Even among those who admired or were fascinated by Japan in the nineteenth century, few were prepared to admit it might, even in the distant future, enjoy equality with their own countries. The views of Bousquet, a French legal adviser to the Japanese government in the 1870s, may have been a little extreme, but many would have subscribed to them:

The Japanese can easily assimilate our industrial knowledge and learn the functioning of our machines, the use of our mechanics, but they are incapable of mastering our

Ornamental carp *(above right)* are prized for their beauty rather than their flavour.

sciences of reason, our higher mathematics, law and philosophy, and our analytical methods are inaccessible to them as long as they are dependent on their own language. . . They can without difficulty become masters of all the material side of our civilization; but as to the intellectual and moral baggage which are the honour of the Aryan races, they must leave them aside, due to an improperly educated brain and a language incapable of assimilating them.

Technology and the legacy of the Industrial Revolution had made it much harder for visitors from the self-professed developed world to perceive Japan as anything other than backward, however charming they may have found its people and customs. Where, after all, were the imposing symbols of progress that the cities of Europe and America were beginning to take for granted? Where were the bridges and viaducts that the engineering acumen of Brunel and his like had made possible in Europe? Where were the trains and railway tracks that now criss-crossed Europe and North America? And where was the confident urban architecture of banks and businesses that proclaimed stability and efficiency to the inhabitants of London, Melbourne and New York alike? It was not long, of course, before all these things were to be seen in Japan, but few Western observers dared to predict that Japan might rapidly catch up with the industrial West.

Nevertheless, Japan continued to hold the fascination of the streams of visitors who passed through Yokohama and Kobe in the nineteenth century and felt impelled to commit their impressions to paper. For many it was the quaintness, the exoticism, the oddness, or the singularity (to use some of their own words) of Japan that appealed most strongly to their sensibilities, and these were qualities that also appealed to their reading public back home. This was apparent from the rapturous reception that greeted Gilbert and Sullivan's *The Mikado* at its première on 14 March 1885. The chorus, after all, sing the following lines:

If you want to know who we are,
We are gentlemen of Japan:
On many a vase and jar –
On many a screen and fan,
We figure in lovely paint:
Our attitude's queer and quaint –
You're wrong if you think it ain't, oh!

An article in the *Fortnightly Review* went even further:

All who love children must love the Japanese, the most gracious, the most courteous, and the most smiling of all peoples, whose rural districts form, with Through-the-Looking-Glass-Country and Wonderland, three kingdoms of merry dreams.

The desire to romanticize Japan in these and other writings about the country is clear; it did not necessarily contradict notions of European superiority. Why should there have been a tendency to romanticize Japan? By and large it can be put down to the feeling that Japan represented a pre-industrial idyllic innocent state; not one to which industrialized countries which had benefited from 'progess' could return, but one which aroused feelings perhaps of nostalgia or wistfulness. For this reason the romantics among the visitors tended to hope that Japan would be preserved in all its innocence for the entertainment of European visitors. One writer in 1878 put it this way: 'Will not the distinctive charms of Japanese life and manners within a few years disappear for ever beneath the monotonous surface of modern civilization?' This was by no means a minority view. For many, the attempts of Japan to train engineers, to construct railways, and to acquire the trappings of an industrialized country were a matter not for congratulation and enthusiastic support but for unashamed regret. As a result they gave short shrift to the industrializing energy of Japan in the late nineteenth century. Notorious in this respect was Isabella Bird, the indomitable traveller who relished hardship. No sooner had she reached Japan in 1880 than she plunged into the untamed interior for months of privation in the belief that this was the way to discover the 'real Japan'. In one sense it was, of course, but any armchair traveller in England or America who read her account and assumed that this, and this alone, was the 'real Japan' would have been as wrong as some fictional Japanese reporting on the Scottish Highlands or, say, Kentucky during the Industrial Revolution.

More than anything else it was the Russo-Japanese War of 1904-5 that brought European and world images of Japan sharply and painfully up to date. Japan had already by this time defeated China in the Sino-Japanese War of 1894-5 and had even become for the first time the equal partner of one of the great powers when the Anglo-Japanese Alliance was concluded in 1901. *The Times* was confident at the outbreak of war in 1904 that Britain had made the right choice of ally in the Far East and that other countries had simply failed to take Japan seriously:

We as a nation alone appear to have formed a shrewder estimate of the Power which has in Eastern waters a naval strength superior to our own, and which at a pinch can put half-a-million of men into the field. But for the rest, they still were pleased to look

*Opposite* A bamboo grove – sub-tropical and temperate rain forest is found in the southern part of Japan, principally on the islands of Honshu, Shikoku and Kyushu. Bamboo is used to make many everyday products from tea-whisks to garden fences.

Japan is a mountainous country with great natural beauty. Rich forests, including bamboo groves, flourish except at very high altitudes.

upon the Japanese through the eyes of the aesthetic penman, and thought of the nation as a people of pretty dolls dressed in flowered silks and dwelling in paper houses of the capacity of matchboxes.

In fact, even the British military observers who were attached to the Japanese once hostilities had begun only became convinced that Japan would win after they had arrived and seen things for themselves. It required perspicuity, not just the affections proper in an ally, to slough off the Japan of *The Mikado* and recognize it as a nation of growing industrial and military power.

The overwhelming Japanese victory in the war with Russia replaced the image of fairyland Japan and prompted some sober reflections in Europe. After all, the European had for the first time been beaten at his own game by an Asian, and for many the realization was not just unpalatable but frightening, and it fanned fears of the mysterious 'Yellow Peril'. At its most extreme, 'Yellow Peril' was the fear of Asiatic hordes descending on Europe – whether they were Japanese or Chinese it mattered not. Some felt that 'the Europeans, disregarding the consequences, have armed the land which one day will fill them with terror'. Asia for the Asians, would, it was feared, be the first step, signalling an end to European imperialism and posing a threat to European civilization itself. The economies of the West could be thrown into disarray by 'Yellow Labour', the plentiful and cheap supply of workers whose products might flood the markets of the West at competitive prices. For all these reasons, there was a strong feeling that any Japanese threat to the established balance of power would be catastrophic. 'There cannot be a world power which is other than white. Any deviation from this principle is the sure way to Armageddon', wrote one observer reflecting on the possibility of Japan aspiring to become a world power.

The racial angle was particularly noticeable on the West Coast of the United States, where the 'Yellow Peril' vision was tied to rising unease about the growing though still small Japanese community of immigrants in California. In 1905 the San Francisco *Chronicle* launched a series of articles directed against the Japanese, or 'the little brown men' as they were described. Readers of what was an influential and respected newspaper were greeted with headlines such as: 'Japanese a Menace to American Women', 'Brown Men and Evil in the Public Schools', 'The Yellow Peril – How Japanese Crowd Out the White Race', and 'Brown Artisans Steal Brains of Whites'.

The *Chronicle* was a Republican newspaper, but anti-Japanese racism was as strong on the American left. A writer in one socialist journal felt that feelings of brotherhood towards the Japanese could not be nurtured 'until we have no longer reason to look upon them as an inflowing horde of alien scabs'. He would clearly have agreed with Jack London: 'I am first of all a white man and only then a Socialist'. In the years after the Russo-Japanese War the possibility of a Japanese invasion of the West Coast of America began to be raised in newspapers and novels, and also in films: *Shadows of the West* (1920) depicted Japanese immigrant farmers in California as spies posing a threat to the nation and sexual predators lying in wait for innocent

Wartime propaganda – this cartoon by Vicky depicting the savage Japanese soldier was published in the *News Chronicle* in 1942.

23

Mount Fuji is Japan's highest mountain at 12,395 feet. It is seen here from one of the five lakes that surround it. The mountain, famous for its beauty and symmetry, is a dormant volcano and last erupted in 1707.

white girls. In the 1920s pressure began to build up in California for the exclusion of Japanese immigrants. There was a 'Swat the Jap' campaign in Los Angeles intended to make life uncomfortable for local Japanese residents and the courts were finding even second-generation immigrants 'aliens ineligible to citizenship'. Finally in 1924 an Immigration Act was passed in Congress specifically excluding Japanese from any further immigration to the United States.

These negative and hostile reactions to Japan grew stronger in the 1930s and developed into the wartime images of propaganda, with varying

degrees of accuracy: the Japanese as butchers, as fanatics, as suicidal maniacs, as inhuman animals of war. But propaganda would not be doing its job if it was fair-minded, and Japanese wartime propaganda was full of similarly bloodthirsty images of Britons, Americans and Australians.

In the years after her defeat Japan spawned yet another family of images to fit the post-war economic 'miracle'. Kimono and Mount Fuji began to appear alongside some of the symbols of industrial development, like sprawling factories and the Bullet Train; groups of Japanese tourists venturing overseas with their new-found affluence but tamely following their guides became stock cartoon figures. There is a measure of truth in some of these images, of course, but they tend to support the feeling that Japan is and always will be bizarre and incomprehensible. The images may have changed, but the clichés remain the same.

A good example is the so-called 'economic miracle'. The years since Word War II have seen Japanese industry rise from shattered foundations to a position in which it is at the forefront of technological development and challenging its competitors. Its growth has been symbolized and publicized at various stages along the way – by the 1964 Olympics, which brought the famous Bullet Train to the attention of the world, by Expo'70 in Osaka, which demonstrated Japanese industrial confidence and technical sophistication, and the Expo '85 in Tsukuba, which brought the new 'science city' there and Japanese innovation to world attention. Japan's economic development since the war is clearly not of the kind that can be confidently put down to the Japanese being good copiers; as one journalist put it after a visit to the science city and the Expo:

> No longer are Japan, and the broader region of East Asia, on the periphery of scientific and technological developments; they must now be included in the heartland. No longer can we speak, in anything but a historical sense, of 'Western' science and technology, for it is now truly a world affair. Lingering doubts of Japanese creative abilities, which are remarkable for their endurance in the face of massive evidence bespeaking exceptional creative power, must now, belatedly, be laid to rest.

It is only too clear that Japan's post-war growth is no miracle. Miraculous it may seem to have been to the Western countries that have hitherto dominated the world economy during the course of the twentieth century, but only to the extent that Japan's economic development before the war has been forgotten. After all, who now remembers where the 1940 Olympics, scheduled to follow the notorious Berlin Olympics of 1936, were to be held before the outbreak of war in Europe necessitated their cancellation? And who remembers the city granted the right to stage an international exposition in the same year? It was Tokyo in both cases.

Japan is certainly a difficult country to understand. This is largely because it has gone its own very separate way for most of its history. That history has few points of contact with the historical traditions of the West, and some understanding of it is indispensable. The images and clichés we are used to are convenient and interestingly exotic, but they are no substitute for knowledge of the Japanese past and appreciation of the way it has shaped the present.

## CHAPTER TWO

# Japan and the Outside World

Rice is the staple of the Japanese diet. Farms are small as arable land is in short supply in this mountainous land. The busiest time of the rice-farming year is early summer when the seedlings are planted out into the waterlogged paddy fields.

For most of the long span of Japanese history the countries that have been important to Japan have not been Europe and America but her close neighbours, China and Korea. It was only in the nineteenth century that Japan's horizons began to reach beyond Asia, to Europe, Australasia and North America and that it looked to the West for guidance and inspiration as well as supplies of materials and technology. Even then, it was China and Korea that continued to obsess Japan well into the twentieth century. The impact that the outside world has had on Japan, from the times it was heavily dependent on China right up to modern times when it first came into contact with the West, has varied enormously and has made it the hybrid mix that it is today.

Once the rice plants are mature the water supply to the paddies is cut off and harvesting begins in the early autumn. Fields are often carved out of the mountain sides to increase the area of land under cultivation.

Japan's contacts with China stretch back into prehistory, but the ethnic origins of the Japanese lie elsewhere. So much is clear from their two very different languages. If Chinese is an essentially monosyllabic language relying not on inflections but on word order to convey meaning, Japanese is exactly the opposite, a highly inflected language with numerous endings and grammatical particles to indicate the relationship between words and to make meaning possible. In so far as language can be a guide, it seems that the roots of the Japanese people are to be found in more northerly parts of Asia where languages that have some similarity to Japanese are spoken, like

Korean and Mongolian. But in spite of the fact that Japan and China were worlds apart in terms of language and ethnic origins, it was from China, either directly or by way of Korea, that Japan derived some of the main elements of its culture. Wet-rice cultivation is a prime example of this.

If neat paddy fields cut into a hillside and bowlfuls of rice seem quintessentially Japanese now, that is a testimony to the impact rice has had on Japanese civilization. But rice was not native to Japan. It was an import, in all probability from southern China. Rice-growing reached Japan about 2,000 years ago, along with metal-working skills in iron and bronze, which provided the means of forging weapons as well as agricultural tools. It was in Kyushu, the island closest to the Asiatic mainland and in the best position to maintain contacts with the outside world, that the early Japanese first attempted to cultivate rice in paddy fields. By the fourth century AD rice-cultivation had reached the Kanto plain, where Tokyo and its satellite cities now leave little room for paddy fields, and by the end of the twelfth century it had spread to the northern extremities of Honshu, the main island.

Rice became the staple item in the Japanese diet, the one indispensable item in a meal. The word for 'rice' in Japanese is often used to mean simply 'meal', and leaving even a few grains in your rice bowl at the end of a meal is considered bad manners. Every home has its own electric rice-cooker and it is used for rice and rice alone. When an American cake-mix company tried to market a form of cake-mix that could be used in rice-cookers at a time when very few Japanese possessed ovens, it met with overwhelming resistance from consumers and the project was a complete flop. In the Japanese diet rice is more important than bread or potatoes are for Europeans and Americans, and the company had failed to take account of that and of the irrational feeling that the rice would be contaminated if the cooker were used for anything else.

The influence of rice extends far beyond the supper table. When first introduced to Japan, rice turned communities of hunters and gatherers, who were dependent on locally available resources like berries or sea-food, into settled agricultural communities that could ensure their own steady supply of food.

The cultivation of wet-rice requires a measure of social organization. Paddy farming demands intensive labour involving the whole community. Much of the work was organized on a cooperative basis and influenced the way of life in rural Japan. Not only did rice dominate the farming year, it also dominated the annual cycle of ceremonies and festivals. Each phase of the rice cycle had its own dangers; the ditches might fail to keep the water at the required level, the seedlings might suffer in a late frost or storm, pests or a typhoon might destroy the crop when it was about to be harvested. So it became the custom, particularly at anxious times of the rice year, to make invocations to the spirit-world in the hope of gaining protection from disaster, and then of holding festivals to express a communal sigh of relief over dangers past.

China contributed much more than rice to the emergent culture of Japan. During the first centuries of the Christian era Japan was in its infancy but China had already matured into a technologically and socially sophisticated state. China had long enjoyed a form of centralized government with bureaucratic local government, systems of laws and taxation that were applied throughout the empire on a standardized basis, rich traditions of literary, philosophical, political and scientific writing, and even a civil service examination system. China was the 'central kingdom' in the contemporary world of east Asia. Peripheral countries, which to Chinese eyes were barbarian lands, were expected to accept and indeed welcome the Chinese world order in which they lived, and for the most part they did so. Chinese writing, philosophy, political institutions, and even Chinese ways of telling the time and the years became standard in Korea and the other surrounding countries. These countries were no match for the military strength of the Han dynasty which ruled over China at this time, and, therefore, had no choice but to submit.

As an island country off the shores of China, Japan was in a favoured position, for it was not directly threatened in a military sense. Nevertheless, the Han dynasty (AD 24-220) and its successors had too much to offer Japan to be ignored. So it is from these early centuries of the Christian era that the first documentary evidence of Japan comes, in the form of references in the Chinese chronicles. The Han historians thought of Japan as the land of dwarves or the land of eastern barbarians, but as good bureaucrats they dutifully recorded what they knew of the country and its people. A number of Japanese communities, they wrote, had been keeping in regular contact with the Han court and were prepared to pay tribute and thus accept the inferior status accepted by China's neighbours. The people, they also noted, were fond of alcohol but there was very little theft and they were reluctant to resort to legal action. In those respects at least the Japan described by the Han historians is recognizable even today, for many a Western visitor has been struck by those very same features in contemporary Japan.

In the fifth and sixth centuries Korean and Chinese immigrants to Japan brought knowledge of Chinese characters and literature as well as Buddhism. Writing had been unknown to the Japanese and the first step towards the development of a system for writing their own language was naturally that of learning to read and write Chinese. But the Chinese writing system was anything but a convenient one for Japanese, hence the complex compromise that written Japanese is today. The problem was that the two languages were completely dissimilar, and so real ingenuity was needed to adapt the Chinese script for the writing of Japanese.

An alphabetic system would have been much more accommodating for an inflected language like Japanese, but chance dictated otherwise. Contact with China took the Japanese language in different directions, gave it an inappropriate writing system and introduced Chinese words and phrases on a large scale. Japanese without Chinese characters and vocabulary is unthinkable today. It is this that makes the task of learning the language such an onerous and time-consuming one for Japanese schoolchildren and foreigners alike. Rote-learning of the characters, their pronunciations and their meanings is an inevitable and important part of primary education,

*Opposite* Calligraphy is a means of communication as well as an art. The Chinese characters are written from top to bottom and then right to left. A Japanese child has to learn many hundreds of characters and two alphabets – here children at primary school practice their calligraphy.

The Japanese adopted the Chinese script many centuries ago although their language is very different. Today neon lights are used for advertising side by side with more traditional signs. Words are often written in Roman letters and a back-street alleyway can display a jumbled mixture of signs – such as this one where several bars and clubs have also opted for foreign names in an attempt to be stylish.

and it is not until you enter your teens that you can begin to think of reading Japanese with ease.

Japan without Buddhism is also unthinkable. Buddhism reached Japan in the sixth century as a sophisticated religion with elaborate rituals and a canon of scriptures in Chinese translation. It was completely new to Japan, which before then had only had the Shinto religion, an intellectually less demanding religious tradition without metaphysics, scriptures or organized clergy. Buddhism quickly found acceptance in Japan, partly because its very differences from Shinto made it less of a threat. It was supported by the early Japanese state, which saw in Buddhism a protector of Japan's still fragile civilization, and it began to influence styles of architecture and art and to import a less worldly philosophic stance that had a lasting effect on literature.

From this time onwards, Japan adhered to a course which was closely tied to China. Contacts with the mainland were kept up not only by immigrants but also by embassies dispatched from time to time to the courts of successive Chinese dynasties. The scholars, monks and officials who made the hazardous voyage to China came back with first-hand knowledge of life and institutions in contemporary China and much of what they had learned was put to work in Japan. There were also Chinese and Korean immigrants in Japan, who brought with them intimate knowledge of Chinese civilization. Among other things, a system of court ranks based on the Chinese model was adopted; and in the seventh century the process went still further when a serious attempt by Japanese reformers was made to remodel their country in the image of China.

This was a project grandly conceived. The object was to introduce the legal system of China, which involved not only the codification of law but the standardized application of it throughout Japan. In addition, the system of land-tenure was adopted which called for all land to belong to the crown but to be parcelled out according to need and to be redistributed from time to time. The attempt was courageous, but without an established and trained bureaucracy and the necessary means of communication it had as little chance of success as a rice-seedling in an English field. But the fact that the attempt was made at all is an indication of the esteem in which Chinese civilization was held at this time.

But the project involved more than laws and land-tenure. Japan lacked a stable capital city and the obvious Chinese model was Ch'ang An, the capital of the T'ang dynasty. Ch'ang An had a population of one million and was the largest city in the world in its day. Japan's new capital city, Heijo-kyo (now Nara) was established in 710, and its successor Heian-kyo (now Kyoto) in 794. Both were modelled on Ch'ang An, as also were the Korean capitals: they were all rectangular in shape, laid out on a grid plan, with the palace on the northern edge. Ch'ang An had a university so Nara and then Kyoto had to have universities. The city gates to Kyoto bore Chinese names, ceremonies at court were conducted after Chinese examples, and poets wrote in Chinese.

The priests' graveyard at a Buddhist temple. Every town in Japan has several Buddhist temples.

*Above* Statues of Jizo, the Buddhist god of children and of the unborn child. These are carved stone statues, sometimes found by the roadside to commemorate the memory of a lost child. In some cases these statues are put up in memory of aborted babies.

*Opposite* Inside a shopping arcade, a small Buddhist altar is tucked away among the shops and is used by shoppers and shopkeepers daily.

The Heian period (794-1185) began with the same reforming policies. Missions were sent to the court of the T'ang, but as the ninth century neared its close the T'ang dynasty (618-906) began to fall into terminal decay. The last Japanese mission left in 838, and those that were planned to succeed it never took place for news of the chaos then in China was reaching Japan. But it was not simply that the ambassadors were becoming afraid for their personal safety: there were already signs that shaping Japan to fit the Chinese model was not working. A reaction had set in against excessive reliance on China and Japan was beginning to do things its own way.

Japan was not and could not become China. Japan did not have traditions of bureaucracy and meritocracy to rely on to form the backbone of an impersonal and centralized form of government. Instead, it had a hereditary court nobility with entrenched interests as well as a powerful Buddhist church with aspirations to political influence. The nobility and the Buddhist church had not opposed the attempt to remake Japan in the image of China, but they had not lost their control of land or their power. Although all land was supposed to belong to the state and to be available for redistribution, in practice the estates of the most powerful bodies were allowed to remain as tax-free anomalies.

*Left* A Buddhist priest sits in the posture normally adopted for meditation.

*Below* A school visit to the Todaiji Temple in Nara. This is the largest wooden building in the world and houses Daibutsu, a colossal bronze statue of Buddha cast in the eighth century when Nara was Japan's capital city.

Japan, during this time, therefore, saw much of its Chinese character disappear. The land system fell into disorder as more and more of the so-called state land passed into private hands and out of the jurisdiction of tax inspectors. The bureaucracy suffered the same fate. Securing a good position no longer depended on merit or whether you were a graduate so much as on whose son you were. The Heian period marked not only an end to Japanese diffidence in the face of China but also the resurgence of confidence in Japanese tastes. The language of poetry was now Japanese, both in the literal sense and in the sense of its inspiration and imagery. The same was true of art which turned from landscapes inspired by Chinese tastes to domestic interiors that were unmistakably Japanese.

The end of the Chinese experiment did not, of course, spell the end of Chinese influence. Neither was contact with China lost altogether. Monks and traders continued to make the hazardous sea-crossing, but for several centuries the influence of Chinese civilization on Japan was muted. During the Kamakura period (1185-1333) travelling monks brought Zen, a new form of Buddhism to Japan, which was to become one of the leading schools of Buddhism in Japan.

The head priest in his country temple. A priest's life is a busy one conducting daily services, comforting the sick, holding funeral services and teaching, together with all the duties involved in running a temple.

Zen was an austere form of Buddhism characterized by the practice of meditation in the difficult lotus posture, itself deriving from Indian traditions of yoga. The Zen temples in Japan flourished under the patronage of the shoguns, who were the hereditary military rulers of Japan from the twelfth to the nineteenth century, and they played an important role in introducing various aspects of contemporary Chinese culture to Japan. Chinese styles of calligraphy, painting, and literature as well as new interpretations of Confucian political philosophy entered Japan through the medium of the Zen temples. They were also at the forefront of new developments in the arts of both peace and war, from the tea-ceremony to swordsmanship. Either directly or indirectly, the traditions associated with the Zen monastic complexes of medieval Japan took root in the country and shaped some of the aesthetic tastes that seem to us today most characteristic of Japan, such as rock gardens and ink paintings.

Contacts with China were broken once again at the end of the thirteenth century. By 1279 the Mongol hordes under Kubilai Khan had overrun China and were threatening Japan. In time the Mongol empire contracted again and its leaders were succeeded as rulers of China by the emperors of the Ming dynasty (1368-1644), who encouraged Japan to resume trading

Three generations of priests praying before the altar in a Buddhist temple. The priests of some Buddhist sects are permitted to marry and often pass their offices on to their sons.

relationships. The Japanese responded favourably and the fifteenth century saw the resumption of full diplomatic contacts between the two countries. The new Ashikaga family of shoguns dispatched official embassies to China which served to confirm their legitimacy, and the shoguns were even willing to accept the controversial title of 'King of Japan'. This title infringed the prerogatives of the emperor and imperial court in Kyoto; not only that, in the context of the Chinese world order, it implied an inferior status with regard to the Chinese emperor – Japan had never been very happy about acknowledging that it was subordinate to anybody.

In the sixteenth century Japan's world expanded with dizzying rapidity. Europeans arrived in Japan and the Japanese discovered the world beyond China to the south and the southwest. By the end of the century Japan had gained so much in international confidence that Hideyoshi, the civil dictator, launched an abortive campaign to vanquish China and Korea. He boasted in letters to his mother that she would soon be seeing her son crowned emperor of China and Japan. But within 50 years Japan had brought down the curtain on its brief flirtation with international life and had entered a period of almost complete seclusion from near and distant neighbours alike. What had happened to bring about such a change?

The garden of the Moss Temple – or Saihoji – in Kyoto. This garden is completely covered by more than 100 species of green and yellow mosses. Kyoto has many fine temples, shrines and palaces with elaborate gardens. It was the capital city of Japan from 794 to 1868.

The Portuguese had discovered Japan in 1543 and had soon introduced the country to Christianity, to the new technology of firearms, to exotic Western dress, and to foreign travel and exploration, which had hitherto been the monopoly of the dreaded Japanese pirate fleets. The prospects for the missionaries looked good and in 1549 St Francis Xavier arrived to begin the work of converting the Japanese to Christianity. He and his fellow Jesuits applied themselves to the task of learning the language and set about producing grammars and devotional works in Japanese for their own use. They even brought a printing press to Japan to print some of these works. They made many willing converts, established churches, and found favour with the authorities, particularly because of the Portuguese traders who often accompanied them.

The Portuguese Jesuits and traders had been followed by Spanish Franciscans and traders, and there seems to have been some friction between the two. Hideyoshi scented danger, perhaps because he feared that missionaries would be followed by colonists or perhaps simply because he feared the effect that large numbers of Japanese Christians might have on social stability. At any rate he issued some edicts against the Christian missionaries. They were not acted upon at first, but they were the harbingers of much worse to come: the expulsion of missionaries, the destruction of their churches, and the execution of converters and converted alike.

It was partly due to the growing persecution of Christians in late-sixteenth-century Japan that Japanese communities began to develop overseas. Japan's growing participation in the international world at this time was not just a matter of an influx of curious foreigners, for Japanese were also settling overseas in significant numbers for the first time. These Japanese communities developed partly as a result of the more adventurous entrepreneurship of individual merchants and also as a result of the exodus of Japanese Christians from Japan prompted by the growing persecution. The settlement in what is now Manila in the Philippines seems to have numbered 3,000 by the early seventeenth century, many of whom were Christian exiles, and there was a large trading community in Thailand which came to play a prominent part in local politics too. There were other communities in Tourane, which became famous as Da Nang during the Vietnam War, Macao, Jakarta and Taiwan. But all this was an Edwardian summer, a last international fling before the Tokugawa shoguns in the 1630s moved to cut off most contacts with the outside world and to impose a strict measure of isolation. It is not too fanciful to see the extent of Japanese trading activities in South-East Asia in the sixteenth and early seventeenth centuries as a sign of growing Japanese confidence at playing an international role; nor to see the trade in raw silk thread and silk cloth (for import), and copper and Japanese craft-ware (for export) as a precursor of the contemporary trade patterns whereby Japan imports raw materials and exports electronic goods. In the years before World War II there were attempts to see Japan's history of involvement in South-East Asia as a justification for Japanese interest in the affairs of its Asian neighbours.

By the time that the Dutch and the English arrived in Japan to set up business in 1600, the Spanish and the Portuguese were already well

The tea-ceremony: at its best an elegant ritual in tranquil and simple surroundings. Originally inspired by Zen this artistic discipline is still widely taught today. It can take several years to learn all the movements of the ceremony, to make the tea correctly, and serve it in the prescribed way.

ensconced and unwilling to see their monopoly on Japan encroached upon by newcomers. It was thanks to the diplomatic skills and pertinacity shown by an English Master Pilot, 'Will' Adams, that the monopoly was broken. Through his efforts both the Dutch East India Company, who were his employers, and later the English East India Company were allowed to establish trading stations at Hirado, a port to the north of Nagasaki.

'Will' Adams lived on in Japan until his death in 1620. After he had become one of the advisers of the shogun, Tokugawa Ieyasu, he had been forbidden to return home to England. He had a country estate as well as his

*Right* Elegant utensils are an important part of the tea-ceremony: (from left to right) a lacquered tea container, a tea bowl, a bamboo whisk and scoop. The tea is thick and green and is drunk as it is after eating a sugar-sweet to counteract the bitterness.

house in Edo (the Tokyo of today), he wore Japanese clothes and spoke Japanese, and he is reputed to have married a Japanese woman by whom he had two children. There can be little doubt that he was not only the first Englishman to visit Japan but also the first to settle in any Asian country. As such he is an intriguing figure, and one that has inspired at least six novels. The first was a romantic and fantastic biography published in 1861, just three years after a treaty had been signed between Japan and Britain re-establishing trade relations after an interval lasting more than 200 years. In the 1980s he became better known in the guise of John Blackthorne, one of the central characters in James Clavell's bestselling novel, *Shōgun*.

In spite of its connection with the romantic figure of Will Adams, however, the English trading house at Hirado was not a commercial success. It had only been in operation for 10 years when orders came from the English East India Company in 1623 for the operation to be brought to a close and the staff to withdraw. One of the main problems had been marketing, as, of course, it can sometimes be today more than 400 years later. The manager of the trading house, Richard Cocks, knew what would sell in Japan: he needed stocks of spices, metals such as lead, tin, and iron, and 'pictures, some lascivious, others of stories of wars by sea and land'. But his requests for supplies of these items fell on deaf ears, and the bulk of his stock consisted of English woollen cloth that he could find no market for in Japan; since he and his staff clothed themselves in silk it was difficult for their customers to take their sales-talk seriously.

So the English pulled out in 1623. By this time the persecution of the missionaries and their converts was entering its most harrowing phase. Richard Cocks wrote with horror of the sights he saw in 1619:

43

> I saw fifty-five martyred at Miyako (Kyoto), at one time when I was there, because they would not forsake their Christian faith, and amongst them were little children of five or six years old burned in their mothers' arms, crying out, 'Jesus receive their souls'.

The missionary effort in Japan was anything but discouraged in spite of the constant loss of both converts and missionary fathers alike, but proselytization was simply becoming more and more difficult as the anti-Christian edicts were enforced. Spaniards and Portuguese, whether traders or missionaries, were barred from Japan and those who remained risked death. By 1640 it was only the Dutch who were allowed to maintain their precarious position in Japan insisting that they were traders pure and simple and had no interest in the Catholic missionary enterprise.

So from 1640 onwards, Japan was for some 200 years almost cut off from most of the outside world. Japanese were forbidden to travel overseas, and if they did so faced the death penalty on their return. The narrow windows on the world that Japan did keep open proved to command a surprisingly wide perspective under the circumstances. Firstly, contacts with China, Korea and the Ryukyu islands continued as before. These were on a modest scale and were strictly supervised, but the maintenance of even minimal trade and diplomatic relations in East Asia gave the Tokugawa shoguns the patina of international legitimacy they sought.

Then there were the Dutch. They were happy to renounce any Christian ambitions in Japan; nevertheless the Japanese authorities were still suspicious of the motives of all Europeans and confined the Dutch trading mission to a tiny manmade island in Nagasaki harbour called Deshima. The island was a rectangle measuring roughly 600 feet by 180 feet and it was surrounded by a high fence. To make the Dutchmen feel even more welcome there was just one small bridge connecting the island with the mainland and this was guarded by sentries at both ends. There were seldom more than 20 Dutchmen on Deshima at one time but there was a swollen Japanese bureaucracy to interpret for them, to cater to their needs, and to keep a close eye on their activities – the Dutch incidentally, had to pay the salaries of all these official hangers-on. The pleasures of this place were well described by the Swedish botanist Karl Thunberg who was sent to Deshima by the Dutch East India Company in 1776:

> A European condemned to spend the rest of his life in this solitude would truly be buried alive, news of great upheavals of empires never reaches this place. The journals of Japan and still less those of foreign countries do not arrive here. One can vegetate here in the most absolute nullity, foreign to all that is taking place on the world scene.

Deshima was off-limits to ordinary Japanese, with the sole exception of Nagasaki courtesans, for the Dutchmen were not allowed to bring their wives with them. As one nineteenth-century inmate put it, 'How then could the Dutch residents otherwise manage to procure any domestic comfort in the long nights of winter, their tea water, for instance, were it not for these women?'

Deshima was an unprepossessing place and promised little as a window on the world for Japan or as a window on Japan for Europe. But, miserable

*Opposite* The rock and sand garden at the Ryoanji Temple in Kyoto. The art of gardening with rocks and stones was introduced by Zen monks.

A view of Nagasaki in the late nineteenth century. Oura Catholic Church, the oldest Gothic-style wooden church in Japan, can be seen in the foreground.

as the lives of its temporary inhabitants may have been, it was through Deshima that Europe learned what it knew of Japan in the eighteenth and nineteenth centuries and that Japan learned of Europe. The first stage for the Japanese was learning the Dutch language. Knowledge of Dutch spread from the official interpreters and grew more sophisticated in the eighteenth century; the only European books reaching Japan at this time were in Dutch, to suit the needs of the residents of Deshima; Dutch was, therefore, the language to learn if you wanted access to foreign books. As a result those eager for knowledge of the West fell into the mistake of assuming that Dutch was a more international language than indeed it was.

What did Europe learn about Japan through Deshima? The mainstay of the unprofitable Dutch operation at Deshima was porcelain and lacquerware – if the word 'japan' was used in eighteenth-century England it usually referred not to the country but to lacquer; to say that something had been 'japanned' meant that it had been lacquered in the Japanese way. Japanese lacquer and porcelain thus made their way into the homes of the prosperous classes in Europe. Several of the heads of the Dutch factory, or the doctors attached to the Dutch settlement at Deshima, also wrote books about their experiences in Japan; these became the only sources of information about contemporary Japan available in Europe from the 1640s onwards. Some of these were translated into English, but did not make much impact.

Much more information passed the other way, from the outside world into Japan. The head of the Dutch factory was required to make an annual expedition to Edo for an audience with the shogun – at his own expense, of course. The presence in Edo of a party of Dutchmen always attracted those with a taste for the exotic and these visits became a regular opportunity for the exchange of information. More important perhaps were the annual reports which the head was required to make to the shogun's government; these were not simply commercial reports for they encompassed current events in Europe and thus kept the shoguns better informed of European events than European rulers were of Japanese affairs. Later, such knowledge was to prove of crucial importance, for example, at the time of the First Opium War (1840-2). The war had been fought by Britain to defend the right of British merchants to sell opium in China and by China to prevent the import of a drug that was clearly having disastrous social consequences. The outcome was inevitable given the technological superiority of the forces at Britain's disposal, and China was forced to cede the territory of Hong Kong and to pay indemnity. News of what had happened to China as a result of its attempt to resist the depradations of the Western powers served as a powerful reminder of the fate Japan too could meet if it handled the Western threat without great care.

At the start of the eighteenth century the Dutch began to play an important role as interpreters of the Western world to Japan. In 1716 a new shogun, Yoshimune, was appointed who began to relax the strict surveillance that had hitherto been placed on the activities of the Dutch and to seek information actively himself. Through his interpreters and advisers, Yoshimune sought information on a variety of subjects that revealed how much Japan had fallen behind in its knowledge of the West since the Portuguese and Spanish had been expelled in the first half of the seventeenth century. On their visits to Edo the Dutch were constantly pestered for things they did not have and were requested to bring them on subsequent visits. They were asked for pictures of European ships and information on shipbuilding, to demonstrate how to fire a pistol while on horseback, to put on a suit of Western armour and walk around in it, to arrange for an expert in the craft of watchmaking to come to Japan with a supply of watches, to have various seeds and plants brought to Japan so that attempts could be made to grow unfamiliar plants like coconut palms and nutmeg trees. The Dutch went to considerable lengths to meet the shogun's demands. He demanded, for example, that they arrange for some horses to be brought to Japan in the Dutch ships regularly calling at Deshima and that some Dutch riding instructors accompany them to offer instruction in equestrian techniques. The most bizarre aspect of this rash of interest in the West was the eating exhibitions held in the shogun's palace in Edo. The Dutchmen were ordered to bring all that they would need for the preparation and consumption of a Western meal, from ingredients to table and table cloth. They were then ordered to prepare a meal and consume it in front of their inquisitive audience. Everything, from the ways in which they used their knives and forks to eat their meat and drank their wine out of glasses, was carefully watched. On other occasions they were asked to bring samples of Western foods, or to send the shogun Spanish wine and some sweets.

Behind all this were clearly some curious minds, and minds which had no memory of the West to call on. What had been learned about Europeans 100 years earlier had slipped out of the collective memory and had to be relearned. Nevertheless, the renewed interest at the highest levels in the manners and knowledge of the Dutch signalled an end to official xenophobia and set an example that many were ready to follow. This new trend became known as 'Dutch learning', despite the fact that some of the most influential heads of the Dutch factory were Swedish or German rather than Dutch and some of the books that circulated in Japan were Dutch translations of German works. Dutch learning did bring a great deal of Western scientific knowledge to Japan, and in due course this had the effect of helping to undermine the prestige of Chinese science and hence of China itself.

There was one other avenue through which Japan learned a little about the outside world and vice versa, and that was from Japanese castaways. Since the laws of Japan at this time were more concerned with the preservation of Japan's controlled seclusion rather than the safety of men at sea, ships could only be built to small dimensions, so as to prevent the possibility of foreign trade and contacts. If a storm arose and a ship was blown far from the coastal routes around Japan, it was in many cases at the mercy of the elements. This was the fate of Denbei, a man of humble birth shipwrecked off Kamchatka, the strategically important Siberian peninsula to the north of Japan. He was taken to St Petersburg and presented to Peter the Great in 1702 and three years later he was ordered to set up a school to teach Japanese. This was the first systematic attempt to teach Japanese outside Japan and although the Russian students were not diligent in their studies, the school survived until 1816. There were enough Japanese shipwrecked off Kamchatka to keep the school properly staffed, but since they were castaway fishermen, and most of them illiterate, it is not surprising that standards at the school were indifferent. Even those Russians who did manage to learn some Japanese would have found it hard to communicate with Japanese people, for they could only speak the country dialects taught them by their teachers. Another reluctant Japanese visitor to St Petersburg, Captain Kodayu, made an impact on fashionable St Petersburg society in 1791 after he and his crew had been shipwrecked. Kodayu was a cut above the normal run of castaways, for he could hold his own in foreign company, and he also kept a diary of his time in Russia.

The experiences of Kodayu and other Japanese shipwrecked on Russian territory were important for two reasons. On the one hand they prompted the Russian government, then expanding its authority eastwards, to look beyond the coasts of Siberia and to consider establishing relations with Japan. This led to Russian expeditions to Japan in 1792 and 1804, ostensibly to return castaways but in fact to explore the possibility of trade with Japan. They were unsuccessful, but they are an early indication of Russian

Japan's scenic coastline. Sailors were often shipwrecked and blown far from Japan's coastal routes and it was partly from their experiences that the country learned about the outside world in the seventeenth and eighteenth centuries.

interests in the Far East. On the other hand, Kodayu and the others provided the shogun's government and scholars of Dutch learning with priceless first-hand knowledge of the West as seen through Japanese eyes. Kodayu, for example, was subjected to what would now be called an extensive debriefing designed to prise out of him every sliver of knowledge he might have; he had after all spent nine years in the society of Russians. He could provide valuable information about billiards, soap, and sedan chairs, as well as matters such as armaments and armed forces, and Russia's intentions in the Far East. But he knew too much for his own good: such intimate knowledge of a foreign country, and one seeking contacts with Japan, made him a victim of concern for national security and he was given a pleasant prison in which to potter around for the rest of his days.

Kamchatka may have been an inhospitable place to be shipwrecked, but at least it was close. That could not be said of North America; the Japanese shipwrecked there had mostly endured long spells adrift at sea without provisions and great hardships before being cast ashore. Captain Jukichi, for example, set sail in October 1813 on a routine coastal voyage with a crew of 13; a storm disabled his ship. They drifted helplessly for a year and a half, dying of malnutrition and sickness one by one, except for Jukichi and two

49

Nineteenth-century technology reached Japan in a rush from the West. Here modern-day industrial development on Amakusa island in Kyushu provides a contrast with the island's history, for it was the setting of a Christian rebellion in 1638 which left many thousands dead.

others who were rescued by a passing ship and taken to California. There they were appalled by the sight of cows being slaughtered for human consumption: meat was simply not eaten in Japan. They were even more shocked on their return to Japan in 1817 to be thrown into prison after a long and arduous homeward journey. Once they had told the authorities all they had seen they were finally allowed to return to their home-town.

In the nineteenth century Japan found itself increasingly the object of unwanted attention from the Western world. Foreign ships often appeared in Japanese waters, and some of them had the effrontery to ignore the seclusion edicts and enter Japanese ports, admittedly to return castaways. The attention was not surprising in the circumstances. Russian ships were busy exploring the eastern edges of Siberia, establishing settlements there and transporting supplies, especially to the fur-trading settlements in Alaska, which was not sold to the United States until 1867. Supplies were a serious problem: the Trans-Siberian railway was yet to be built and there were no Russian ports on the Siberian seaboard that were free of ice throughout the year. There would be no problem, of course, if Japan put an end to its seclusion and opened up its ports.

While Russia was looking eastwards America was looking westwards. The push from New England to the west had reached the shores of the Pacific: eyes were already being focussed on the opposite shores of the Pacific, on the lucrative China trade. Japan could serve as a bunkering station for American steamships, which in those early days could not traverse the Pacific with ease because of the vast stocks of coal they had to carry. Shipwrecked American whalers also focussed attention on Japan. Public feeling was that they had not been treated as well as shipwrecked sailors deserved. Britain and France were also toying with the idea of making approaches to Japan at this time, though in Britain the unprofitable years in Hirado were still a strong-enough memory to make the venture seem only moderately promising. Nevertheless the prospect of trade with Japan was beginning to arouse the interest of several nations: indeed to a world firmly committed not only to the principles of free-trade but also to the belief that trade was in itself beneficial and desirable, it was an affront to see a country like Japan refusing to cooperate.

In 1853 the United States sent Commodore Perry to Japan with the object of bringing the nonsense of seclusion to an end. There was no secrecy about the expedition, and as soon as word reached St Petersburg the Russian government decided to launch its own expedition under Admiral Putyatin. Perry reached Japan a month before Putyatin, made his demands, warned that he would be back the following year with a much stronger force to receive the answer and then left to winter in Hong Kong. Putyatin, meanwhile, was continuing his negotiations and was finding some grounds for optimism when, early in 1854, the Crimean War broke out and he had to flee: a combined British and French squadron was on the look-out for him and he sailed to the safety of Kamchatka.

The Japanese government had been thrown into consternation by the arrival first of Perry and then Putyatin, but it knew all too clearly that Japan's defences were no match for Perry's well-armed fleet of steam-powered men-of-war. What is more, news of China's humiliating surrender after the First Opium War had long since reached Japan and induced a mood of sombre caution. So when Perry returned early in 1854 he found little inclination to resist American demands and he took a treaty back home with him. Before leaving he impressed the Japanese negotiators with American technology: they were fascinated by the model train which puffed its way around a track and by the demonstration of how it was possible to send messages along pieces of wire.

Later in 1854 Britain, France and other countries secured treaties with Japan; early the following year Putyatin secured one for Russia. That treaty had been delayed by the Crimean War but it was the most worth while, for it opened more ports to Russian ships and allowed for more Russian consuls in Japan than did any of the other treaties. These treaties established the rights of foreign ships to call at Japanese ports and of foreign diplomatic representatives to reside in Japan, but not much else. They did not confer the right to trade, but they were a start.

Townsend Harris arrived to act as America's first diplomatic representative in Japan, and set up his office in a converted temple. It was a dangerous time for foreigners in Japan: for each enthusiast eager for knowledge of the West there was a fanatic convinced that foreigners were polluting Japanese soil.

Negotiations with the shogun's government were excruciatingly difficult but Harris and the other foreign diplomats persevered with them in order to procure the right to trade in Japan. This issue of trade was settled in the treaties of 1858, known in Japan as the infamous 'Unequal Treaties'. They were unequal in several senses. Tariffs, for example, were fixed at a low rate indefinitely – the Japanese government had no control over its own tariff rates charged on foreign imports and could not protect its own fledgling industries.

The adminstration of law was another controversial area. Foreigners were to be exempt from Japanese law and could only be tried by consular courts, even for serious crimes. A notorious case involved a British ship, the *Normanton*, which sank in a storm in 1886 off the coast of Wakayama. Captain Drake and his English crew took to the lifeboats and escaped, leaving all 23 of the Japanese passengers to drown. The captain and crew had to answer for this not to a Japanese court but to a consular court, which cleared them of all charges. Such was the public outcry in Japan that a new trial was held in the British consulate in Yokohama. However, Drake was only sentenced to three months' imprisonment and no compensation was paid for the loss of the lives of the Japanese passengers.

Abandoning seclusion had dire consequences in Japan. It embroiled the shogun's government in domestic political strife from which it was unable to extricate itself and which resulted in its final collapse in 1868 when the emperors took over government once more. It also set in motion changes that were to have an effect on Japanese society very few predicted in the 1850s.

Nineteenth-century technology reached Japan in such a rush that misunderstandings were inevitable and knowledge about the life and institutions of the countries that had introduced these technologies to Japan was at a premium. It is hard for us now to realize just how ill-informed about the West even the most educated and sophisticated Japanese were at this time. For example, the members of Japan's first overseas mission, to America in the summer of 1860, acquired a taste for champagne during their stay in New York but on one occasion they were frightened to discover hard objects floating in their glasses. These objects were nothing more than lumps of ice, but it had simply not occurred to them that ice could be procured in America even in the summer. They did not know what to do with their chamber pots either: they found them under their

*Opposite* A girl dressed up for the Seven-Five-Three festival, when girls of seven and three and boys of five and three are taken to a Shinto shrine where they will be paraded and photographed and perhaps blessed as well. Shinto is a religion that demands little of its adherents and festivals such as this are more social occasions than religious.

beds in their hotel rooms and it was only after extensive discussion that they finally agreed that they must be pillows enabling them to preserve their elaborate samurai hair-styles while they slept.

On another occasion a ball was held in honour of the embassy at the grand home of the Secretary of State, Lewis Cass. The senior members of the embassy were, of course, the guests of honour, but they had not the faintest idea of what was going on and were baffled by the entire evening, and particularly by the dancing. The senior Japanese present was the ambassador, Muragaki, and his diary carefully describes what he saw without evincing any understanding of what it meant:

> Men and women moved round the room couple by couple, walking on tiptoe to the tune of the music. It was just like a number of mice running around and around. There was neither taste nor charm. It was quite amusing to watch women's skirts spread wider and wider like balloons as they turned. Apparently, high officials and older women, as well as young people, are very fond of this pastime. . . . It is indeed odd that the Prime Minister [sic!] should invite an ambassador of another country to an event of this sort. My sense of displeasure is boundless: there is no respect for order and ceremony or obligation. The only way to exonerate them is by recognizing that all this absence of ceremony issues from their feeling of friendship.

The other members of the embassy were just as bewildered by the occasion: their hosts may have thought they were doing their visitors proud, but the Japanese visitors for their part could not suppress the feeling that entertainment was an inappropriately frivolous form of diplomatic ceremonial. Another shock for them was to observe the behaviour of Americans in the presence of their President. How could he be as important as he was supposed to be, they wondered, if he dressed in a plain suit without the splendour that to their eyes was an indispensable badge of rank, and why did his subjects not prostrate themselves before him to show the awe in which they held him? If Muragaki and his companions did not understand the nature of political authority in the United States, they certainly did not understand the process of electing the President. For them this seemed to be some kind of auction.

A more serious misunderstanding occurred when nineteenth-century Japanese converts to Christianity supposed that the Christian nations of the West would live up to their name and behave fairly and honestly in their dealings with Japan. It may have been naive of them to entertain such ideas but it nevertheless came as a considerable shock to some to discover how important a factor national self-interest was in nineteenth-century international relations. There can be no doubt that it occasioned some disillusionment with the ideals the Europeans and Americans had encouraged Japan to adopt, and it also brought to an end the 20 years of success enjoyed by the Christian missions in Japan since the early 1870s. The exposure to the West changed the trickle of information passing through Deshima into an unmanageable flood; even Commodore Perry found the Japanese he had to deal with in 1854 insatiably curious about all that was new to them, from the uniforms of the American sailors to the steam engines that propelled their ships.

Despite rampant Westernization in the cities the rural areas of Japan continued to lead a more traditional way of life. Rice farming changed little over the centuries. In spring the paddy fields are ready for the transplanting of the rice seedlings.

The thirst for information was satisfied in various ways. Those who had been abroad could write of their experiences, as Fukuzawa Yukichi did in his bestseller, *Conditions in the West*. In the 1870s Japanese translations of legal textbooks, Disraeli's novels, and Samuel Smiles' *Self-Help*, began to appear at random. The enthusiasm of those days, the confidence in newly acquired Western tastes, and the shaky understanding are all well captured in an extract from a satire published in 1871. The speaker is a Japanese dandy in one of the new beef restaurants; he maintains an up-to-date air by ostentatiously drawing out a Western pocket-watch to consult the time as often as he dare:

> Pretty good stuff this beef, don't you think? Can't think why we've never eaten it 'till now, nothing wrong with it after all. Japan's really getting a bit of civilization now, and it's a good job that we're getting to see some of the beef too. Course there are still some blinkered types around who blather on about eating beef being a barbaric custom, making you unclean and unfit to pray, and all that. It's all because they don't know anything about science.

They do everything by logic in the West, you know, you've got to hand it to them. Steamships, steam engines, can't beat 'em. Balloons to bring winds down from the sky, now isn't that an invention?! Course, the point of them is this. Take a map of the world and there are some countries in the middle marked 'tropical', right? Now that part is called the equator. It's where the sun shines closest and the heat is something terrible. So the king there tried this and that and finally came up with balloons, big round bags they are, which you fill up with winds. When you get them down from the sky you open them up and all the winds spread around making it cool again. Some idea, eh?

Just as Japan had taken China as a model a little over 1,000 years earlier, so now Japan was taking the West as its model. Top-knots, swords and kimonos were exchanged for short haircuts, top hats and frock coats. This even applied to the Emperor. The Emperor Meiji was not the secluded figure his immediate predecessors had been; instead, he was dressed in Western-style military uniforms and became a public monarch. The leading politicians were setting a similar example at the Rokumeikan. The Rokumeikan, in English the 'Deer Cry Pavilion', was built in 1883 by a British architect as an entertainment centre for the new Japanese government. It was full of billiard rooms and ballrooms, and the drinks, the music and the dress were all Western. So was the company, for those who frequented the Rokumeikan followed Western practice in taking their wives along as well. There was even a grand fancy-dress ball there in 1887 attended by the Prime Minister dressed as a Venetian nobleman. This was civilization as Muragaki and the other members of the Japanese mission had found it in Washington in 1860.

One of the motives for the rampant Westernization of the 1870s and 1880s was the desire to be rid of the 'Unequal Treaties'. Japan would only be able to do that, it was felt, once she had been accepted as a civilized equal by the United States and the European powers. Dressing Japan in Western clothes seemed to be the answer, but the fancy-dress ball had a whiff of scandal about it and it marked the end of the popularity of the Rokumeikan. Not only that, the sad decline in the popularity of the Rokumeikan symbolized another change in Japanese sentiments, one like the trend against things Chinese in the Heian period 1,000 years earlier. The basic goals remained the same: the creation of a strong army to guarantee Japanese independence and of a firm industrial base for the economy. The technology too would continue to be that of the West, but the notion, popular earlier, that things Western were intrinsically superior was no longer accepted unquestioningly. Japan in the 1890s was seeking to find its own place in the international society of the late nineteenth century, just as it is today.

The history of Japan's relations with the outside world is one of great fluctuations. At times Japan has been dazzled and captivated by the new worlds it has come into contact with. At other times it has withdrawn into itself, to digest and absorb the unfamiliar dishes it has tried to consume. Europe and America came into this process only recently. Although their relationships with Japan in the space of just a century or so have been stormy, they are only a small part of Japan's long historical traditions.

*Opposite* A family portrait in the nineteenth century – 'top-knots, swords and kimonos were exchanged for short haircuts, top hats and frock coats'. On formal occasions the men wore Western dress while the women dressed traditionally in kimonos.

## CHAPTER THREE

# Japan at War

Our attitudes in the West towards Japan are still strongly coloured by World War II. Memories of the Bataan death march, the Burma railway, the massacres of civilians at Hong Kong and the executions of prisoners of war are as emotive reminders of brutality as the names of the most infamous Nazi concentration camps. Nobody on the Allied side can be surprised that the memories and feelings of bitterness of the wartime generation have in many cases changed very little with the passing of the years. Nor is it surprising that the Emperor's visit to England and Holland in 1971 aroused such strong reactions; after all, he was the same Hirohito who had been the Japanese bogeyman of Allied propaganda during the war. For the same reason the Dutch government in August 1986 cancelled plans for a visit by Queen Beatrix to Japan: the memory of the deaths of many Dutch men and women in Japanese internment camps during the war makes Japan still a sensitive issue in the Netherlands. On the other hand, Queen Elizabeth II and President Reagan, as well as successive British and Australian Prime Ministers, have been able to visit Japan without arousing storms of protest for many years now.

The post-war generations of Europe, America and the Pacific know nothing of the war at first hand. But books such as *King Rat* by James Clavell, who was himself a prisoner of the Japanese in the infamous Changi Jail in Singapore, have passed memories of the Pacific War on to a generation that never experienced it. So too have films such as *The Bridge Over the River Kwai, Tora! Tora! Tora!,* and more recently *Merry Christmas, Mr Lawrence*, as well as the popular British television series *Tenko* about the experiences of prisoners in the Japanese prisoner-of-war camps. Many Japanese find it surprising and even annoying that the Pacific War continues to be such a part of the consciousness of their wartime enemies.

Nobody reflecting on the Pacific War today can find anything to excuse the brutality of man to man, and nobody can preach forgiveness to those who suffered or to their friends and relatives. But that does not mean that the Pacific War should remain a closed book. Far from it. The war was, as everybody knows, a cataclysmic clash of Japan with the English-speaking world, but it was also a war in which colonialism, racism, and Japan's perceptions of its place in the world had important parts to play. The war is still a taboo subject when a Westerner meets a Japanese, but that taboo needs breaking, in the interests of understanding Japan's position in the world as the twentieth century draws to a close.

Wartime propaganda made the Japanese out to be a nation of people so intrinsically warlike and violent as to be almost inhuman. The impression that the Japanese are an essentially warlike people is supported by one of the most potent images of Japan in the West, that of the samurai; an image that conjures up the fear and awe felt by visitors to Japan in the 1850s as well as the fanaticism of the Japanese army during the war. The samurai is

The samurai warriors were easily identifiable by their distinctive dress and the exclusive right to carry swords. This photograph was taken in a studio in the 1870s just before the samurai lost the right to wear their two swords in public. The studio backdrop shows Mount Fuji.

59

the initial skirmishing after the landing in northern Kyushu the Japanese had the worst of the fighting: the invaders had deployed in disciplined groups making skilful use of bells and gongs as signals and frightening the defenders with their use of gunpowder, which was then unknown in Japan. But the prayers were answered and Japan saved, for a gale blew up at night and wrecked much of the fleet, drowning up to a third of the troops.

This was not enough to deter Kubilai Khan. The following year more envoys were sent to Japan with the same uncompromising message, but the *bakufu* (military government) confidently beheaded them as they did subsequent envoys too. The second invasion came in 1281. This time there were two fleets, carrying a total of 140,000 men, and they were successful in establishing a beach-head. By comparison, the Spanish Armada when attacking England in 1588 had less than a tenth of the ships and manpower of the Mongol fleet. However, after two months, the best part of the fleet was destroyed by a typhoon and the invasion force was compelled to withdraw with great loss of life.

Kubilai by no means gave up his plans to invade Japan even after this second disaster, and several times he had preparations begun for a third invasion, but they came to nothing. Japan had been saved by the wind, but by no ordinary wind. These winds, it was thought, were the work of the Ise shrine – they were divine winds, in Japanese *kamikaze*, that had saved the nation in its hour of need. More than 600 years later, when Japan was staring defeat in the Pacific War in the face, hopes were again pinned on *kamikaze*; but this time, rather than leaving nature to do its work, the task was entrusted to suicide pilots. The idea was that they would be able to rescue Japan in its hour of need just as the real *kamikaze* had done at the time of the Mongol invasions.

Unfortunately, the very success of the samurai armies which had rallied to the flag to repel the Mongols left the shogunate with a dire problem, that of how to reward those who had served the nation well. There were no spoils of war and no lands to confiscate, but there were a lot of people clamouring for rewards for their services and becoming increasingly dissatisfied by their treatment. This unhappy situation hastened the end of the Kamakura shogunate, which was replaced in 1333 by the Muromachi shogunate, based in the Muromachi quarter of Kyoto. The Muromachi shoguns presided over a period of political fragmentation and lawlessness which culminated in the devastation and carnage of the Onin War of 1467-77.

In spite of the violence of the age, the arts flourished in the Muromachi period. It was a period in which the samurai patronage of the arts and learning inspired a rich harvest of gardens and paintings that are still among the highpoints of any visit to Japan. One example is the Ginkakuji, or Temple of the Silver Pavilion. This was a retreat built in the eastern hills of Kyoto by the shogun Ashikaga Yoshimasa: the pavilion was never covered in silver, though its cousin, Kinkakuji, the Golden Pavilion, was covered with gold leaf, only to be burned down by a deranged monk in the 1950s.

The chaos and political fragmentation lasted until the end of the sixteenth century. Japan was carved up into what were to all intents and purposes separate princedoms, each under a daimyo or baron who owed

The sword was the symbol of the samurai class. Here samurai are seen wielding their swords during the civil wars of the fourteenth century under the Muromachi shogunate.

allegiance to nobody and sought to protect and extend the area under his sway. The second half of the sixteenth century was dominated by the emergence of several figures who were seeking a more ambitious goal, that of unifying Japan under their own leadership. One was Takeda Shingen: in Kurosawa's recent film *Kagemusha* his death is kept secret by the use of a 'double', who acts the part of Shingen so as to avoid destroying the morale of his troops. But Shingen's effort was doomed by his failure to appreciate the importance of firearms.

The five-storied keep of Himeji Castle on Honshu in western Japan. Himeji is regarded as the most beautiful castle in Japan. Castles were built as the seats of the daimyo and Himeji dates from the Azuchi-Momoyama period at the end of the sixteenth century.

Firearms had been introduced to Japan in 1549 and had rapidly spread throughout the country. They were at first used as an adjunct to the more conventional weapons of the samurai, the sword and halberd. But at the battle of Nagashino in 1575 Oda Nobunaga used them with devastating success as the lynchpin of his strategy, and the result was the utter defeat of Shingen's armies. From then on firearms were an indispensable part of warfare as Nobunaga extended his control over most of central Japan. Nobunaga's attempt to unify Japan under his sway came to a suitably bloody end when Akechi Mitsuhide, a treacherous follower with ambitions of his own, launched a sudden attack and Nobunaga was assassinated. Akechi's success was short-lived, for within a year he had been defeated in battle by Toyotomi Hideyoshi. Later Akechi's head was put on public display, a grisly but effective equivalent of a press release to say that Hideyoshi was taking over where Nobunaga had left off.

Hideyoshi had risen from very humble birth to being one of Nobunaga's leading generals and he managed to subdue the outlying parts of Japan that Nobunaga had left untouched at his death. Having established a fragile peace throughout the land he began to turn his attention to the mainland. In 1592 he launched an invasion of Korea. The invasion force of over 100,000 men made rapid and destructive progress up through the Korean peninsula to Seoul and beyond. In occupied areas the Japanese commanders encouraged the local inhabitants to learn Japanese and to identify themselves with Japan, though with little more success than in the twentieth century. However, sickness, the winter frost, constant guerilla attacks, the arrival of reinforcement armies from China to help the Koreans defend their country, and a series of naval disasters gradually undermined the Japanese position in Korea and as soon as Hideyoshi died in 1598 the Japanese armies were withdrawn.

Was Hideyoshi mad? Many have thought so, and some certainly said he had been possessed by a fox, which was a polite way of saying so. Many of his letters, however, survive, and they show a mind that is not so much deranged as supremely confident, as the following extract shows:

> I intend to cross over to Korea during the 3rd month. Also, a report has come saying that the envoys who have come from China to apologize have arrived at the harbor of Korea and are waiting for a favorable wind, so if I go over to Korea, I shall be back in triumph shortly.

It is true that the plan to invade China after Korea smacks of delusions of grandeur. Hideyoshi had known nothing but military success so far in his confrontations with local Japanese warlords, but China was a foe of quite a different order and the invasion had as much chance of success as the attack on the United States in 1941. All the same, an invasion of China would have been unthinkable before the time of Hideyoshi and it was a sign that Japan in the sixteenth century was beginning to develop its own ideas of international society in the East, ones that were not dependent as hitherto on China but gave Japan a central role to play.

On his deathbed Hideyoshi had begged all his generals to be loyal to his son, Hideyori, who was only five years old. He wrote the following letter just over a month before his death to five of his most powerful lieutenants: it was on their cooperation that Hideyori's succession depended. 'I repeat: concerning the business of Hideyori. I am begging and begging the five of you. The details have been conveyed to the five Commissioners. I am loath to part. I end here.' Hideyoshi was clearly a desperately worried man. He had good reason to be, for, as he feared, the five did not keep their word once he was dead. Hideyoshi had established no machinery of government that might survive his death and ensure Hideyori's succession when he came of age, and it was clear once he was dead that there would be a period in which his leading followers, nominally the guardians of Hideyori's interests, would jockey for position and in time resort to arms. The leading contender from the beginning was Tokugawa Ieyasu, who had enjoyed an income and personal estates greater even than Hideyoshi's.

The trial of strength came just two years later in 1600 when Ieyasu and his supporters met their opponents, who claimed to be protecting the interests of Hideyori, at Sekigahara to the west of Nagoya. Ieyasu's victory gave him military domination over the entire country.

After the battle of Sekigahara, Ieyasu established a new line of shoguns that was to last over 200 years until 1868. He had created the conditions of peace, but maintaining it posed intricate problems. Another problem was that of the succession, which neither Nobunaga nor Hideyoshi had managed to ensure for their heirs. Bureaucracy is not the stuff of adventure stories and is never associated with great generalship, but it was the creation of the bureaucratic society that enabled Ieyasu to convert his victory in 1600 into the foundations of a lasting regime. The first task was to eliminate any military threats to his position. Hideyori's days were, of course, numbered, and in 1615 Ieyasu laid seige to Osaka Castle, which was the base of Hideyori and his supporters. The outcome was Hideyori's suicide at the end of the seige, and thus the end of the house of Toyotomi. In the process of achieving this Ieyasu had broken all the promises he had made to Hideyoshi, but he had ensured now that no challenges could come from the Toyotomi family. Ieyasu died the next year, but he had long since taken steps to ensure the succession of his son.

The settlement that Ieyasu and his descendants imposed on Japan in the early seventeenth century was a shrewd compromise. The daimyo were allowed to retain control over local affairs in their fiefs, even those who had fought against Ieyasu. But Ieyasu meant his regime to last and for that it was important to ensure that the daimyo would not be able to cherish greater ambitions. This required ensuring that they would be too weak economically and militarily to be able to mount a credible challenge to the Tokugawa shoguns. Weakening the daimyo economically proved easy. They were required, for example, to keep up a flow of presents to the shogun's household, and a close watch was kept to make sure that they were spending suitably large sums on the presents. They were required also to make an annual journey from their home to Edo which was the seat of the Tokugawa shogunate and which changed its named to Tokyo in 1868. The daimyo had to reside there for half the year, which entailed substantial travel expenses in addition to the cost of maintaining another home there,

The keep of Himeji Castle from the outer defence works. The castle is also known as the White Crane Castle with its white plastered walls, buildings and towering keep at its centre.

and here too they were required to do things in style. Furthermore, they had to destroy all their castles except their official residence and, to forestall the use of marriage as a means of contracting alliances, they had to submit their marriage plans for the shogun's approval.

So much for possible rivals, but for centuries much of Japan had been an armed camp, and there were in the early 1600s large numbers of soldiers who were old campaigners and had seen service either at home or in Korea. They had no lands to work or any other occupation, so how were they to be absorbed into a new society based on the arts of peace rather than war?

The solution was to make them into a kind of governing class, to translate them from warriors to bureaucrats. This did not happen immediately, of course, for Ieyasu and his successors were not so confident of their power as to presume that military strength could be completely dispensed with. Nevertheless, in the course of the seventeenth century the education of samurai for a different role in society came to be seen as increasingly important and the curricula at the samurai schools combined the skills of the soldier with literary skills in the field of Chinese philosophy, which was to the Tokugawa shogunate as Classics was to the British civil service and government in the nineteenth century. The intention was to create what we would today call an all-rounder: he would be acquainted not only with Chinese classical literature but also adept at the use of the sword or the lance. But since there were no wars from 1640 until the 1860s and no opportunity

67

for putting military skills into practice, there was a tendency for those skills to be ritualized and to become of less practical significance. Studies of swordsmanship, for example, became increasingly theoretical and of diminishing use: much attention was paid to ensuring that the footwork and the stance were just right but what was right depended not on wartime experience nor on what would be most effective in combat but on the theories followed by the teacher.

By the nineteenth century the situation in some samurai schools was becoming a matter for serious concern. In one notorious case horsemanship was practised indoors on wooden horses on rainy days. Milksop samurai afraid of getting their armour wet are a long way from our usual images of samurai. They were not all like that in the 1850s of course, as the first diplomats and traders found out when they took up residence in Japan: for some were murdered by xenophobic fanatics who certainly knew how to use their swords, even in the rain. But before the arrival of Perry and Putyatin the shogun's government was seriously worried about the military readiness of the nation's samurai as well as the state of coastal defences; it was all too apparent that Japan was in no position to resist the forces at the disposal of the Western powers in the Far East and would, in the event of war, in all likelihood suffer the fate of China after the Opium War. In the years before the resignation of the last shogun in 1868 the government made attempts to create the kernel of something that could function as an efficient national army. Instructors were brought over from France to train samurai as foot-soldiers, cavalry and artillery officers along European lines, but all this came far too late.

The Meiji Restoration of 1868 brought an end to two and a half centuries of rule by the Tokugawa shoguns with a nominal restoration of power to the Emperor Meiji who was still in his teens. The new goals of the imperialist government encompassed the creation of a nation state with all its trappings, from an education system to a national anthem. An important part of this was a national army to secure Japan's independence. What was revolutionary about the new army was that it was not to be a samurai army so much as a conscript army. After almost 1,000 years, the samurai had lost his claim to be the sole bearer of arms in Japan. The new conscription act was introduced in 1873.

As a class the samurai were on a slippery slope in the early Meiji period. They had lost their monopoly on warfare and were gradually losing their guaranteed incomes and having to fend for themselves, even find jobs. It is not surprising, therefore, that there were several samurai revolts which expressed the resentment and disorientation felt by those unable to adapt to the new world of Meiji Japan. The most important of these was the Satsuma Rebellion, which took place in 1877, the year after the samurai were ordered to stop wearing swords. This gave the new conscript army its first test under fire, and it passed with flying colours. This was the beginning of the modern Japanese army.

Japan had good reason to feel nervous about its security in the late nineteenth century, and so to feel the need to build up a strong army and equally strong navy. Throughout the Far East there was a strong colonial presence

Japan's new army outfought the Chinese in the Sino-Japanese War of 1894-5 – a war fought over Korea. China was so soundly defeated that she conceded Korea's independence and gave Formosa and other islands to Japan.

其ノ八 松崎大尉戦死

飛丸急霰の如く松崎大
尉終に戦死す 征清軍中
第一殉国の思と為す

and it was threatening to expand further. The British were in India and Hong Kong, the French in Indochina, the Dutch in Indonesia, the Germans in China, and the Americans moving across the Pacific first to Hawaii and then to the Philippines. Particularly worrying to the Japanese was the continuing destabilization of China throughout the nineteenth century by the major colonial powers. And then there was Russia to the north, with its

The Himeji Fighting Festival. The palanquins rest on long poles which are carried on the shoulders of the men.

interest in Korea for the sake of a warm-water port in the Far East. The Sino-Japanese War of 1894-5 was fought over the issue of control of Korea and it was at the same time the first successful test of Japan's new armed forces in combat overseas.

In spite of its victory in the Sino-Japanese War, Japan was unable to reap the territorial gains that had been anticipated, on account of the 'Triple Intervention'. In 1895 the governments of Russia, France and Germany 'advised' Japan not to press its claim on the strategic Liaotung Peninsula on

the ground that this would prejudice the independence of Korea. In view of the fact that the Russian Pacific Fleet was in a state of war-readiness, the Japanese government saw no alternative but to renounce its claim. However, the Triple Intervention provoked widespread popular unrest in Japan and fanned the flames of virulent nationalism. This was particularly so after Russia acquired the Liaotung Peninsula for itself in 1898. Russia subsequently developed Port Arthur, at the tip of the peninsula, as its warmwater port in the Far East and effectively gained control over the entire Korean peninsula.

In 1904 the confrontation between Japan and Russia over the Korean peninsula came to a head, and the result was the Russo-Japanese War, which belatedly awakened the European powers to Japan's growing military strength. The war started in a dramatic way in February 1904 when Japanese naval torpedo boats launched a sudden attack on the Russian naval squadrons at Port Arthur and inflicted considerable damage. Japan did not trouble to declare war until several days later, but at the time this did not unduly disturb Western observers. The correspondent of *The Times* wrote that, 'the Japanese navy has taken the initiative and has opened the way by an act of daring'. British and American observers, however, took a very different view of the similar attack on Pearl Harbor in 1941.

The Russo-Japanese War lasted less than two years, but Japan's armed forces, which were now barely a quarter of a century old, managed in that time to inflict decisive if costly defeats on Russia, both on land and at sea. On land each side committed roughly a million troops and the casualties were at a commensurate level: some 58,000 Japanese were killed during the long and terrible siege of Port Arthur, as many as the number of Americans killed during the entire Vietnam War. While the battles were raging on land, the Russian Baltic Fleet was sailing around the world in the hope of regaining the naval initiative, but it was to be decisively outmanoeuvred and torn to pieces in the Tsushima straits between Japan and Korea. A seaman working in the sick-bay on board one of the Russian ironclads later wrote an account of the action that is as horrifying as it is critical of the quality of the Russian commanders:

> We were outclassed by the Japanese in respect of speed and accuracy, in the quality of shells, and in concentration of fire.
>
> An hour sufficed to transform our squadron into a floating caravan of death.
>
> Now the injured were coming or being brought in thick and fast: men with bellies torn open, bones broken, skulls fractured. Some were so badly burned as to be unrecognizable; they shivered pitifully, moaning: 'I'm so cold, so bitterly cold'.
>
> Vasya Drozd, with both legs shot off at the knee, was in the death-struggle. His eyes anguished, his face twisted, he was bounding on the red stumps that were left him, trying (it seemed) to run, and fighting desperately for breath. A moment later he fell into the pool of his own blood.

The slaughter in the Russo-Japanese War was as terrible as this extract suggests: the heavy machinery of twentieth-century warfare was an efficient and merciless killer. Partly for this reason the other major military powers of the world showed as keen an interest in the conduct of the war as

A quiet moment during the Himeji Fighting Festival. The Japanese love festivals and the year is filled with them. All the cities, towns and villages celebrate their own festivals reflecting their history and ancient traditions.

they did in its results. Britain and several other countries sent attachés to both sides to monitor the progress of the war and to learn what lessons they could. They were impressed by what they saw and some said that Japan's greatest triumph was in battle against disease in the field. Afterwards they were eloquent in their praise of what *The Times'* correspondent called Japan's 'noblest triumph' and 'the ability, prudence, and modesty' with which it had been achieved.

For Japan the war had been economically exhausting and the human losses had been great. On the other hand, Russian designs had been effectively checked and Japan had now secured for itself a free hand to extend its control over Korea. In 1910 Japan annexed Korea and began to incorporate it within the Japanese empire. For Korea this was a tragedy: Koreans were forced to take Japanese names and to learn Japanese in schools and they were reduced to the role of passive observers of the fate of their country. But for Japan it was a necessary move: it was now playing the expansionist and colonialist game, though several decades after the European powers had secured their possessions in the East.

For Britons, Americans, Australians and the Dutch, the war with Japan began with the attack on Pearl Harbor in December 1941, but by that time Japan had already been at war on the mainland for several years. Japan's activities in China stemmed from a desire to establish itself as the dominant force in East Asia. It was a kind of insurance policy to safeguard its own position, for Japan continued to feel that the European powers active in the Far East were trespassing in its back garden. The objective was to replace European colonists in Asia with Japanese colonists and reserve the economic benefits of China to Japan alone.

The first opportunity to act in pursuit of these goals came in 1914 with the outbreak of World War I. Japan entered the war on the British side partly on account of the Anglo-Japanese Alliance, which had first been signed in 1902 and subsequently renewed; though Japan, of course, had no intention of sending troops to the battlefields of Flanders. The idea, rather, was to bring to an end Germany's interests in China and to take over German territorial possessions, such as Tsingtao where the best beer in Asia was and still is brewed. Within a few months of the outbreak of war this had been achieved: German troops and warships in the Far East had surrendered to Japan, and it had taken over not only the German possessions in China but also the Mariana, Caroline and Marshall islands in the Pacific which had all been German possessions. But Germany had more important things to think about at this time, as indeed had the other European powers involved in the war. In this respect, World War I was convenient for Japan: its government could refuse to send troops to Europe, and act to improve its own position in East Asia without any real fear of interference.

However, in 1915 Japan's ambitions in China came into conflict with British and American interests for the first time. The Japanese government had presented to China a list of proposals known as the Twenty-One Demands. The matters covered in these Demands included not only the transfer of German rights and concessions in China to Japan but also preferential conditions for Japanese industrialists and financiers operating in

## CHAPTER FOUR

# Information and Technology

*Left* Japanese efficiency at work. A group of construction engineers synchronize their efforts wiring new telephone lines.

*Below* Robots at work in a car factory – the Japanese automobile industry was one of the first to introduce robots and automation into factories. In 1955 Japan was only building 20,000 cars a year but by the mid 1980s it was building 8 million cars a year bringing it on a par with the United States.

'The Japanese are pretty good at copying things, and clever with their hands too; they are an ingenious lot.' Or so went the patronizing assessment of Japan's capabilities until comparatively recently. Anybody now in their thirties or older will remember when 'Made in Japan' was taken to mean cheap and unreliable, but in the face of the evidence opinions have had to be revised. As the ever-growing trade deficit with Japan has made apparent, consumers throughout the world are now choosing to buy Japanese. The recent rise in the value of the yen has made the price of some Japanese goods less competitive than they once were but for quality, Japanese electronic equipment and high-tech goods continue to enjoy the high reputation they have already established for themselves. Brand names like Sony, Honda, Canon, Seiko and Akai immediately spring to the mind of anybody buying a motorcycle, a video recorder, a computer printer, or a new camera. Such is the appeal of the Japanese brand-names that some

*Above* Assembly-line workers discuss production problems with the management. The methods of Japanese management are world-famous. In a crisis managers do not hesitate to join the assembly line themselves. They wear the same uniform as the workers and share the same facilities.

*Opposite* Humidifiers on display in Akihabara, the huge electronic and appliance market place in Tokyo

British and American firms have chosen to give their latest hi-fi products Japanese or Japanese-sounding names.

The strong Japanese presence in the market for luxury and consumer goods is still a relatively recent phenomenon, as is the challenge they have given to European and North American manufacturers. The familiar Japanese brand-names are now being joined by Korean and other Asian brand-names, such as Hyundai in the case of cars and Samsung in electronics, but it was the Japanese that originally led the way and they who continue to be at the forefront of these markets. How did the Japanese, and now the Koreans, master the technologies that Westerners used to think of as their own? The simple answer would be that it was all part of Japan's economic miracle. But Japan has a much longer history of technological development than most users of Japanese cameras and cars would suspect, and it is this that explains much of the Japanese technological prowess in the twentieth century.

Japanese contacts with China more than 1,000 years ago gave technology and science its first real impetus in Japan. Early Japan was enthralled by what it came to know of China in the T'ang dynasty and began to model its social and political organization and town-planning, and even its literature and cultural life, on China. During the heyday of this age of enthusiasm for everything Chinese in the seventh and eighth centuries, many of the fruits of China's long history of scientific and technological development reached

*Left* Wires and cables for the electric apparatus that fills every home. The development of the electrical industry has meant that appliances such as washing machines, refrigerators, television sets and vacuum cleaners are owned by most Japanese households.

*Below* An automatic camera is tested before it is packaged for sale. Japanese cameras have become increasingly sophisticated and feature the latest developments of technology. In Japan everyone has a camera and the Japanese tourist armed with a camera has become a common sight in the West.

Japan. While some Chinese and Korean scholars were coming to settle in Japan, Japanese students were travelling to China and returning with books and first-hand experience of Chinese arts and sciences.

A major accomplishment of this period was one of the world's first exercises in mass production. In the middle of the eighth century there had been some friction between the Buddhist church, the imperial court and the government, and to appease the church, the Empress Shotoku ordered the printing of a million Buddhist invocations. Over the space of six years, from 764 to 770, they were printed on oblong pieces of paper, rolled up, and then placed inside small model pagodas which had been made at the same time in a massive wood-working operation. The pagodas were then distributed in batches of 100,000 to ten of the most important temples in the land. Over the centuries, fire has taken a heavy toll: only a few of those belonging to the Horyuji Temple near Nara have survived today. There are perhaps in all several thousand left around the world, some in the Horyuji and others in museums. The printing was done with wooden blocks rather than with movable type, but all the same this vast printing operation was carried out more than 600 years before Guthenberg started printing in Mainz in the middle of the fifteenth century. No older samples of printing

survive anywhere in the world, with the exception of a single similar Buddhist invocation printed in Korea a few years earlier. The overwhelming probability is that printing was one of the many practices learned from China at this time, but the persecution of Buddhism in China in the ninth century and the ravages of time and the violence attending dynastic changes have left no samples of printing in China dating from earlier than the ninth century. But even if printing was a skill learned from China, it was to be many centuries before printing in Europe became a mass-production industry on this scale.

To encourage the growth of Chinese learning in Japan the court established a university and various institutes. Here Japanese students grappled with Chinese texts on astronomy, medicine, and mathematics. Astronomy was essential for measuring time, for preparing calendars and for interpreting eclipses and other natural phenomena for a superstitious people: as in Europe, early astronomy was closely linked to astrology and to areas of scientific enquiry that are no longer regarded as respectable. Medicine has obvious uses. Chinese medicine was based on speculative ideas of the body and health rather than on empirical investigation of the body's organs by dissection, but there was a large body of literature on bone-setting, acupuncture, herbal remedies and other methods of treatment from the pharmaceutical to the magical. In the eighth and ninth centuries Japanese began writing their own medical books based intitially on the Chinese books they had at their disposal, and these began the long tradition of Chinese medicine in Japan which is still very much alive today: acupuncture and

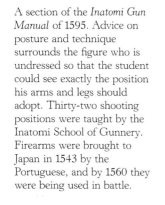

A section of the *Inatomi Gun Manual* of 1595. Advice on posture and technique surrounds the figure who is undressed so that the student could see exactly the position his arms and legs should adopt. Thirty-two shooting positions were taught by the Inatomi School of Gunnery. Firearms were brought to Japan in 1543 by the Portuguese, and by 1560 they were being used in battle.

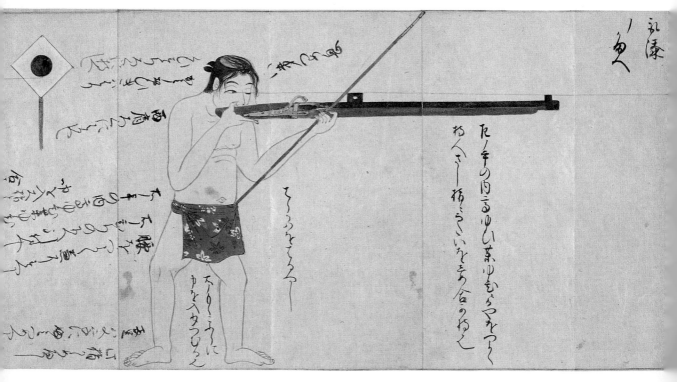

herbal medicines are far from being on the periphery of medical practice in Japan. The uses of mathematics were not so obvious to the Japanese court. As a result, Chinese mathematical traditions attracted only a meagre and short-lived following at this stage, and it was not until mathematics could be seen to answer some of the needs of the bureaucracy that it was given any encouragement. What bureaucrats needed to know was simply enough arithmetic to be able to survey land, calculate taxes and finances, and plan the construction of cities and large buildings.

The end of official contacts with China in the ninth century led to a sharp reduction in cultural links, and, with the exception of medicine, the sciences went into a long decline. Out of touch with what was going on in China, astronomers made virtually no progress and for centuries made do with rough-and-ready calendars. As became apparent later, these had long been superceded in China itself by calendars that required little modification from year to year because they were based on a more accurate measurement of the length of year. The university was also suffering a decline. The Chinese bureaucratic system, based on merit rather than birth, had fallen out of favour and more and more positions were becoming hereditary. Once this trend began to affect the university and the professorship of mathematics became hereditary the decline set in. Thus the university that had been intended to provide a training for government office was fast becoming redundant.

It was not until the sixteenth century that Japan received once more a powerful stimulus from outside. It was then that firearms and the printing press reached Japan and within a matter of years the Japanese were manufacturing these themselves. There is no gainsaying that this was an exercise in copying, but then the first step in acquiring any new technology is to learn how to reproduce it and to do this was no small achievement.

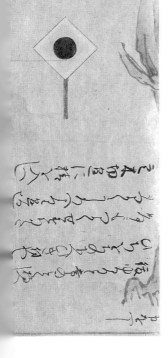

In the summer of 1543 a Chinese junk drifted ashore at Tanegashima, an island to the south of Kyushu. On board were three Portuguese – the first Europeans to set foot in Japan. The local daimyo soon learned that they could bring down ducks out of the sky simply by pointing metal tubes at them and making a lot of noise. The metal tube was an arquebus, a kind of musket, and its impact was sensational. The daimyo asked the Portuguese for lessons in shooting and bought two of the arquebuses for an exorbitant price. He then ordered a swordsmith to make reproductions. The swordsmith managed to fashion several guns within a year and just a few years later production had developed so rapidly that Oda Nobunaga, the first of the three men who sought to unify Japan at the end of the sixteenth century, placed an order for 500 of these new guns. By 1560 firearms were being used in battle and in 1575 Nobunaga employed 3,000 arquebuses for his famous victory at Nagashino: his gunmen were drawn up three ranks deep and each rank of 1,000 men fired a volley in turn with devastating effect on an enemy relying on a samurai charge. Within a few more years firearms were being manufactured near Osaka and elsewhere and were even being exported to China and Korea. The pace was breathtaking, and it was partly fuelled by the incessant civil wars of the sixteenth century and the awareness of the military significance of firearms.

The Japanese are enthusiastic readers; the average household takes two daily papers – the total daily circulation of newspapers being around 44 million copies. Four daily papers are published in English. There are many weekly publications catering for all tastes.

Japan was the only country in Asia to shift rapidly from importing arque-buses to manufacturing them locally. The secret lay in the hands of the Japanese swordsmiths, for the first gunsmiths had all started life as sword-smiths. The quality of Japanese swords had been famed throughout the Far East for well over a century and they were exported in large numbers along with suits of armour. At their best they were far sharper than European blades and could literally cut a European sword in two or cut through a suit of armour.

Thus the techniques of manufacturing high quality steel and forging it enabled the Japanese to manufacture guns. But the first stage of this was to apply the techniques they had perfected for the manufacture of swords to copying the unfamiliar imported arquebuses. Once the swordsmiths had achieved this, they began to introduce refinements and improvements of their own. They improved the trigger mechanism and invented an acces-sory which shielded the matchlock mechanism and so enabled guns to be fired in the rain or at night without giving the marksman's position away.

The gun, therefore, was a sixteenth-century example of successful tech-nology-transfer. But, astonishingly, use and manufacture of the gun fell into a decline in the seventeenth century and by the nineteenth century firearms technology in Japan was way behind that of Europe. Guns under-mined the social order in warfare: the skills needed were easy to learn. As long as the civil wars continued, this situation was accepted in the interests

A typical bookshop in Japan. Many popular Western books are translated into Japanese.

of military success, but once the Tokugawa shoguns had re-established peace and imposed a rigid social order based on the dominance of the samurai class, the gun fell into disfavour: it was no respecter, after all, of rank and so was in effect a subversive weapon.

By the time that well-armed Western ships began to appear frequently in Japanese waters in the first half of the nineteenth century, Japan had only a small stock of antiquated weapons at its disposal. So short was the supply of guns that many old *tanegashima* guns were modernized for use by the new national army in the 1870s, and some of them were even converted a second time and used during the Russo-Japanese War.

The technology of printing was similar in that movable-type printing did not take root in Japan at this stage for reasons other than technological. Over the centuries since the production of the Buddhist invocations, printing had remained largely under the control of the Buddhist temples. Many of the works printed were Buddhist scriptures or doctrinal works, apart from a few medical and Confucian works, and few if any of them were intended for sale or commercial distribution. The process used was woodblock printing, which involved the printing of a complete page from a carved wooden block. The author or a fine calligrapher would write out a neat copy of each page on thin paper, which would then be pasted face down onto the block. The block-carver would carve away the white parts, leaving only the written text standing. Then it was the printer's job to apply ink to the block and press a sheet of paper to it, which produced an entire printed page in one simple operation. Thus the minimum unit was one page, not the individual letter as in the case of movable-type printing.

In the last decades of the sixteenth century printing presses with supplies of movable type reached Japan from two different sources. Jesuit missionaries from Europe set up a printing press in southwestern Japan. At first this was used to print works in the Roman alphabet, either devotional works in Latin for their own use or Japanese works written out in Roman script for the benefit of priests trying to learn the language. These included a Japanese-Latin dictionary and a version of *Aesop's Fables* in romanized Japanese. Later the Jesuits cast some new metal type to print in Japanese, and produced a few works before the press ceased operating.

The other source was a Korean printing press, one of the spoils of war brought back by Hideyoshi's troops after the unsuccessful invasion of Korea. Although originally a Chinese invention movable-type printing was used more widely in Korea. The Korean printing press attracted more attention than the Jesuit press, partly because it did not have the Christian connections of the Jesuit press but also because it was brought to Kyoto, the cultural centre of Japan. Both the Emperor and the shogun became interested enough in printing to sponsor the publication of various philosophical works and also the expensive business of casting new fonts of metal type.

A bookshop in Edo in the early nineteenth century. Japan at this time had a literacy rate that was comparable to that of much of Western Europe.

94

In an attempt to seem fashionable and trendy, foreign names are as popular for magazines as they are for bars and coffee shops.

Their example was followed by a number of individuals or institutions such as Buddhist temples wealthy enough to be able to undertake the expense of preparing a font of type. Among the finest productions of the early seventeenth century when the Japanese were experimenting with movable type were the Saga books. These were a series of works of Japanese literature published in the Saga district of Kyoto by the great calligrapher Koetsu, who designed the type, and a wealthy charcoal merchant who provided the financial backing. The Saga books were often printed on coloured paper, sometimes with stencilled designs, and the finished product was a thing of great beauty.

Movable type remained a popular method of printing up to the 1640s but after that it fell into disuse and wood-block printing came to the fore again. The reasons for this were economic. Publishing was becoming increasingly commercial: publishers were less likely to be wealthy individuals and to be businessmen instead. As such they lacked the considerable capital needed to create a font of type but for wood-block printing they simply had to purchase the wooden blocks and pay a carver to carve out the text on the wood. Furthermore, if they underestimated the demand for a particular work, they could reprint from their blocks whereas movable-type printers had the laborious job of reassembling the type.

The seventeenth century marked a turning point in the commercial history of Japan. By 1700 there were hundreds of publishers operating in Edo (Tokyo), Kyoto and Osaka, and a handful in the provinces as well. There were circulating libraries which would lend books out for a fraction of the purchase price and even bring them around to the homes of their customers. The publishing trade had already organized itself into guilds and begun to publish lists of books in print. What sort of books could you have bought at a contemporary bookshop? Scholars could buy editions of the Chinese classics, priests could buy Buddhist scriptures, and rakes could buy guides to the pleasure quarters, complete with information about all the courtesans, where they were to be found and what their special accomplishments were. If you were bent on self-improvement, you could buy guides to letter-writing and etiquette. If you were only interested in reading for leisure, you would have a vast range to choose from, from current bestsellers, as often as not set in the pleasure quarters away from the watchful eye of the shogun's government, to poetry collections, playbooks and the classic works of Japanese literature like the *Tale of Genji*.

There were also broadsheets to be had from street pedlars. These were the nearest thing Japan had to a newspaper until the nineteenth century, and they served many similar purposes. They told of floods and other natural disasters in the provinces, disasters which could have serious economic implications because they might drastically affect the price of rice in the futures market. They told of fires in the cities, often caused by earthquakes, and marked off the areas on city maps to show which areas had suffered.

So partly as a result of the growth of publishing and the spread of information, Japan developed into a literate society with a national culture. Statistics are hard to come by but it seems likely that certainly by the beginning of the nineteenth century Japan had a literacy rate that was comparable

The medical school at Wakayama on Honshu which was established in 1792. Western medicine had a great impact on Japan in the eighteenth century – knowledge was acquired from the Dutch community on Deshima. The world's first successful operation performed under a general anaesthetic was carried out in Wakayama in 1805 – in the West the first was in 1842.

with that of much of Western Europe and in advance of that of Russia. But science was a different matter. Scientific and technological development received little encouragement from the government of the shoguns and so initially made little headway. However, there was some progress in the field of mathematics, which attained a sophisticated level in the seventeenth century, but in military and medical science, for example, the most important developments were stimulated by the knowledge of Western science which percolated through the Dutch community on Deshima.

The impact of Western medicine on Japan was greatly accelerated by the discovery that traditional Chinese anatomical charts gave a much less accurate picture of the inside of the body than the European charts which had reached Japan. Knowledge of human anatomy was not regarded as important in the practice of Chinese medicine. Executed criminals offered the only chance of making any detailed anatomical study and the first time doctors in Japan were given permission to carry out the dissection of a corpse was in 1754 when some thieves were executed in Kyoto. One of the doctors present wrote an account of the dissection and made it clear that his observations had not tallied with the anatomical charts used in Japan.

This discovery prompted the dissection of an executed prisoner in Edo in 1771 when two doctors were staggered to find that the arrangement of the internal organs spread out before them exactly matched the Dutch anatomical atlases they had brought with them. It was a sensational discovery and it stimulated them to undertake a translation of the Dutch work they had been consulting during the dissection. The publication of this work in 1774 dealt a blow to the prestige of Chinese medicine in Japan and considerably enhanced the standing of what was called 'Dutch' medicine. The popularity of Dutch studies grew and many translations followed of books on surgery, physiology, obstetrics, diseases of the eye, and so on.

Following this, medical practice and knowledge made rapid strides in Japan in the early nineteenth century. One of the most remarkable developments was the world's first successful surgical operation performed under a general anaesthetic. In the West the first operation under a general anaesthetic was performed in Jefferson, Georgia, in 1842, when Dr Crawford Long administered ether to a patient while a colleague removed a tumour from the patient's neck. But in 1805 in the provincial Japanese town of Wakayama, a doctor called Hanaoka Seishu, using a herbal compound to induce total anaesthesia, performed an operation to remove a breast cancer. There can be no doubt that this was the first use of a general anaesthetic in the world, but it is Crawford Long whose name still appears in encyclopedias as the first to administer an anaesthetic. It was also a Japanese who was the first, in 1803, to discover the function of the kidneys; in the West this discovery was not made until 1842 by an American army doctor.

Practitioners of the 'new' medicine grew rapidly in numbers, particularly after the arrival of Philipp von Siebold in Japan in 1823. Siebold went to Deshima as a young doctor determined to learn all he could about Japan and he was allowed considerable freedom by the Japanese authorities to achieve his aims. He set up house not in Deshima but in a suburb of Nagasaki and started giving lessons in the practice and procedures of medicine.

The shipyards of Kawasaki Heavy Industries in Kobe, a seaport stretching nine miles along the coast of Osaka Bay on Honshu. These famous shipyards are among the oldest in Japan and the photograph shows the last commercial ship ever to be built here.

These lectures gave Japanese doctors their first systematic knowledge of Western medical practice and they exerted a powerful influence. When Siebold made a trip to Edo in 1826 he found himself much in demand and consented to give further lectures and demonstrations of surgery. His stay in Japan came to an abrupt end in 1829, however, when a number of forbidden items – detailed maps of the Japanese coastline which were held to compromise Japan's security – were found in his possession and he was expelled from the country.

In the nineteenth century Japan was finding new inspiration in what it was learning from the West. Once Japan had yielded to the pressures

applied by Commodore Perry in 1853 and put an end to the centuries of seclusion, the trickle of information about the West coming from Deshima proved completely inadequate to meet the demand.

At this point the Japanese actively began to seek out knowledge of Western science and technology. Even the shogun's government, which was finding itself increasingly in danger of the collapse that came in 1868, recognized the need for technological reform and paid for a French team to go to Japan and establish a dockyard and workshop in order to train Japanese in the skills of ship construction and repair. American mining engineers were also engaged by the government to investigate mining prospects in Hokkaido and a Briton was hired to manage the development of a coal mine. Some technicians from a Manchester firm helped the local fief government in Satsuma at the southern tip of Kyushu to establish a spinning plant. Alternatively, students were sent to Europe or America, where they were expected not only to master a foreign language but also to acquire, for example, the rudiments of physics or chemistry.

The task that Japan was setting itself was clearly spelled out in Fukuzawa Yukichi's bestseller, *Conditions in the West*, which was first published in 1867. Fukuzawa had travelled as far as San Francisco in 1860 as a junior member of the first Japanese mission to the United States. Fukuzawa encountered much that was new and a cause for wonder and puzzlement. But Japan was not quite as backward as some Americans evidently believed, as this extract from his autobiography makes clear:

> Our hosts in San Francisco were very considerate in showing us examples of modern industry. There was as yet no railway laid to the city, nor was there any electric light in use. But the telegraph system and also Galvani's electroplating were already in use. Then we were taken to a sugar refinery and had the principle of the operation explained to us quite minutely. I am sure that our hosts thought that they were showing us something entirely new, naturally looking for our surprise at each new device of modern engineering. But on the contrary, there was really nothing new, at least to me. I knew the principle of telegraphy even if I had not seen the actual machine before; I knew that sugar was bleached by straining the solution with bone-black, and that in boiling down the solution, the vacuum was used to better effect than heat. I had been studying nothing else but such scientific principles ever since I had entered Ogata's school (a school of Western learning in Osaka).

After the Meiji Restoration of 1868 the new government became strongly committed to the importation of Western technology and to industrialization. As before, this involved both bringing foreign experts to Japan and sending Japanese students abroad, but this time on a much larger scale. The salaries offered to foreign experts were high, high enough to interest thousands in the prospects of a couple of years in Japan whether or not they really had the requisite skills. In the early days before the government became wise to the possibility of fraud a number of nondescripts took office as professors of English. As a contemporary observer pointed out, 'Coming directly from the bar-room, the brothel, the gambling saloon, or the resort of boon companions, they brought the graces, the language and the manners of those places into the school room.'

Inspecting industrial components in a factory. The high costs associated with the rising yen have made Japanese heavy industry less competitive than it was.

But in spite of the occasional unsuitable appointment, the Meiji government continued to employ foreigners in various capacities until the end of the century and beyond. More than 3,000 foreigners came to Japan to work for the government, and most of them were British. There were also large contingents from France, the United States and Germany, and handfuls from Canada, Australia, New Zealand, Scandinavia, China, Korea and Malaya. Almost all of them were drawing salaries well in excess of what they could have commanded at home and at levels that were inconceivable for their Japanese counterparts. All the expenses were met by the Japanese government rather than their home countries. As a result of their high salaries, many acquired somewhat inflated images of their own importance and the value of their contribution to Meiji Japan. It was found that for a new project on average a quarter of the costs would have to be set aside to pay the salaries and expenses of the foreign engineers. There was clearly a strong incentive for the Japanese government to replace this foreign help with skilled Japanese: hence the growing numbers of Japanese students dispatched abroad in the 1870s and 1880s to acquire the necessary expertise and experience.

Many of the foreign employees were brought to Japan as interpreters and translators of English, Russian, French and German, or as language teachers. Many had the roles of advisers on specialized subjects such as international law, several being involved in the process by which Japan gradually acquired the trappings of what the nineteenth-century Western world regarded as 'civilization', such as a code of law and a judicial system, a constitution, a parliament, a postal system, accounting procedures, and so on. For Japan at that time, the acquisition of a European veneer was a matter of overwhelming importance: for, as we have seen, the treaties that had been signed with the Western powers in 1858 denied Japan the right to determine its own trade tariffs on imported goods or to try the cases of foreigners accused of crimes. The only way to reverse these 'Unequal Treaties', as they were widely known, was seen to be the Westernization of Japan. In this way, it was hoped, Japan would eventually be able to show itself worthy of the name of a 'civilized nation' in the eyes of the West and so be trusted to run its own affairs. Some of these hopes were frustrated over the years and Japan did not gain full tariff autonomy until 1911.

In addition to the foreign teachers, administrators and translators, there was also a substantial group brought to Japan for their technological skills. Towards the end of the nineteenth century the Industrial Revolution had transformed the economic and social life of much of Europe. Japan had neither the machine technology of the Industrial Revolution nor the technicians and skilled workforces to operate machinery, and there was little choice but to rely on foreign skills to fill the gap. There was an urgent need for hydraulic, sanitation and construction engineers, technicians familiar with the industrial application of the steam engine, for architects to design Western-style buildings, for surveyors and mining engineers, for telegraphists, and even for photographers, lighthouse keepers and skilled labourers. No Japanese had the ability to put any of these specialized skills into practice, which explains the need also for labourers to work on the construction of the railways.

A nineteenth-century pottery shop. A large range of wares was available for domestic use showing that shops were as sophisticated as their counterparts in the West.

*Above* A woman worker at a factory of Kawasaki Heavy Industries

The Bullet Train, which was introduced at the time of Expo'70 in Osaka, has brought Japanese railways a measure of worldwide fame. The blue and white livery of the sleek streamlined carriages passing in front of Mount Fuji is one of the most familiar and clichéd images of Japan. It has now lost its title of the world's fastest train to the French TGV, but it is still a powerful symbol of the Japanese commitment to railway development at a time when many nations were beginning to close down lines. But the appearance of the railway in Japan came more than 30 years after its appearance in

*Above right* A construction worker off duty. The white overall and headgear are typical.

Europe and America, and the early stages of its development in Japan were at first dependent on imported expertise. The equipment was all imported too, from the railway engines and carriages to the tickets and the peaked caps for the station masters.

The construction of the first line started in 1870 and it was complete in 1872. It ran from Shinagawa in Tokyo to Yokohama, the port where a large part of the foreign community then lived. It aroused a wave of enthusiasm for railway travel from the moment that the Emperor Meiji declared the

Yokohama station in the late nineteenth century. As part of the modernization programme the Meiji government opened Japan's first railway line in 1872. It ran between Tokyo and Yokohama.

line open. The subsequent development of the railway network was rapid. In the 1873 work began on a railway to link Kyoto and Osaka with Kobe, another major port with a large foreign community.

By 1889 the railway covered the 300 miles between Tokyo and Kobe. It followed the old Tokaido route along the eastern seaboard that had once been the subject of some of the finest woodblock prints and was in the twentieth century to become a major industrial belt with the densest concentration of population in Japan. By the early years of the twentieth century most of the country, including all of the four main islands, had been covered by railway lines, some of them private. The trunk lines were nationalized in 1906-7, leaving some private railway companies operating local or commuter lines, a situation that remains more or less unchanged today. As a French visitor to Japan at the time noted, Japan now possessed an impressive railway system:

> The care that the Japanese have neglected to bestow upon their system of roads has been entirely consecrated to their railway system. At the present time Japan is covered with railways, for the Japanese are constantly travelling, and move from one place to another with the greatest ease.

Japan had, of course, long been supplying its own engineers and railway workers and since 1907 it had been manufacturing its own locomotives.

The Bullet Train along with other commuter trains thunders its way into Tokyo. Japan is famed for its efficient and comfortable rail services and runs the world's most tightly scheduled trains.

The network expanded further in the years before World War II, but after the war it was some time before the damage caused by bombing was made good and the railways reached the level of the 1930s. After the initial Bullet Train line connecting Tokyo and Osaka had been opened in 1964 work on extensions commenced: the Bullet Trains run on the standard gauge and require special tracks that can stand the strain of trains travelling at a maximum of 130 mph. Now the Bullet Trains cover several routes in northern Honshu and the main route from Tokyo down to northern Kyushu.

Nevertheless, in spite of the Bullet Train and the experiments with a Linear Motor railway, which travels at a speed of 500 mph and could be the high-tech railway of the future, it is clear that Japanese railways as a whole have passed their heyday and entered a period of decline.

The quality of Japanese consumer goods has indeed risen steadily since World War II. But it has taken a long time to overcome the lingering feeling in the West that Japanese economic success has been built on copying and that the Japanese are not inventive. It has also taken a long time to accept that Japanese science and technology have reached a very sophisticated level. Recently the Japanese 'fifth-generation' computer project, as well as more modest examples of product development, has been drawing close attention, and as a result attitudes have begun to change. In March 1985 the *Far Eastern Economic Review* carried a detailed report of the 1985 World

The Bullet Train or 'shinkansen' first came into service when the Tokaido Line between Tokyo and Osaka was opened on 1 October 1964. The Sanyo Line was completed in 1972 and two new lines in 1982. The fastest service is called 'hikari' (meaning 'light').

Exposition on Science and Technology, which was held at Tsukuba in Japan, and announced on its front cover, 'And now we bring. . . THE INNOVATIVE JAPANESE!' Similarly the *New Scientist* has carried a long report on 'The New Face of Japanese Science' while the *Economist* has had a report on 'The Titans of High Technology', in which it referred to the United States and Japan.

Can the old cliché about the Japanese as good imitators be on the way out at last? The media at least no longer doubt that Japan is innovative; instead they are tackling the problem of trying to explain the phenomenon. As the *Financial Times* put it, 'One of the most challenging conundrums of commerical life is the speed at which Japanese corporations blitz the world's market places with new consumer goods. How is it that rigidly structured companies with hierarchical chains of command . . . can innovate and develop new products so quickly?'

One of the reasons for this 'blitz' is that since World War II Japanese research and industrial development has been far less concerned with military technology than has been true in the West. It has been directed almost wholly towards the development of consumer products. Similarly, academic research in Japan has had a much smaller role to play than industrial research and it is the industrial research laboratories that have attracted many of the best minds of each generation.

Another factor is the role of the Ministry of International Trade and Industry (MITI) in coordinating industrial responses to the challenges of

Crowds board a commuter train during the rush hour. Tokyo's commuter lines and subway system are notorious for the crowds of passengers that squash into the carriages. Some subway stations are linked to the main line train stations.

new technologies. Some writers, particularly those resistant to the idea of a planned economy, have tended to depict MITI as the evil genius behind Japanese economic success, deliberately setting out to wreck key areas of its competitors' economies. A more dispassionate view is that MITI's powers are limited to coordinating and guiding companies down paths they are already prepared to go: steel companies faced with the need to retrench were often unwilling to make the step individually but could act in unison when a strategy for dealing with a declining industry had been drafted by MITI. Crucial to MITI's success has been its uncanny ability to predict world economic trends and to organize the Japanese response; it is this that has been behind the shifts in the focus of the Japanese economy from heavy industry to electronics. In the early 1980s, for example, MITI recognized the future potential of large-scale microchips and mobilized electronics companies to prepare to meet the need, even to the extent of helping to fund their research. So successful was this strategy that within a few years Japan had nearly 30 per cent of the world market for this crucial component of the electronics revolution.

But research budgets and the role of MITI are far from being the whole story. The reputation of Japanese products ultimately rests on the shoulders of a workforce that has had a long education with very high standards in science and mathematics, a workforce that profoundly believes the quality of the work it does every day affects its future, the future of the company it works for, and the future of Japan.

Some have argued that Japanese innovation must be a myth because only four Japanese scientists have won Nobel prizes. However, that is partly a result of the organization of research spending in Japan, for the Nobel prizes for the most part reward university rather than industrial research. Japan's research expenditure has been growing since 1965 at a pace well above that of America and Europe and in total it is now second only to the United States. In Japan, however, about 75 per cent of research funding is provided by Japan's major business companies rather than by the government and

Even the toy shops are high-tech in modern Japan. Since the 1950s, robots have captured the imagination of the Japanese and today toy shops devote ample space to robot displays. There are also shops entirely devoted to these futuristic toys.

Televisions on special offer. Japan was the second country in the world to begin regular colour television programmes. Television sets form a large part of the electronics export industry. With innovative design, high-quality technology, and clever marketing Japan has captured many of the world's markets.

much of the research is carried out in their own laboratories rather than in the universities. As a result, the momentum of Japanese research effort has gone into technology, and especially technology with industrial applications, rather than pure science, which remains the preserve of the universities. Whether Japanese scientists will win more Nobel prizes in the future will perhaps depend on how the universities manage to reverse what Professor Fukui, Japan's latest Nobel laureate, sees as deteriorating conditions for young university researchers. But over the next few years the developments in robotics, micro-engineering, bio-engineering and other fields, which are already being pioneered by Japanese researchers, will leave no room for doubting that innovation in Japan is in a very healthy state.

It may be uncomfortable for Britains and Americans to acknowledge that Japanese science and technology are now innovative rather than imitative, but the fact remains that the next Japanese product they purchase will probably have been invented and developed in Japan rather than copied from the West. This is only surprising to those who are unaware that Hitachi patents more inventions that any other company in the world.

It was on the island of Tanegashima that Japan first came into contact with Western technology in the shape of muskets. It is apt that Tanegashima should now be the location of Japan's space centre and the setting of another exercise in the transfer of technology. The Japanese space programme has enjoyed a series of 16 perfect launches, including the successful launch of its first observation satellite on 20 February 1987. The rockets are still American in design, but by 1992 the Japanese National Space Agency will be largely independent of American space technology and launching its own rockets. Without the long technological traditions which the name Tanegashima represents, the Japanese space programme and technological prowess of the 1980s would indeed be a miracle.

## CHAPTER FIVE

# Town and Country

*Left* Shihjuku, a frenetic business and shopping district in Tokyo by day, turns on the neon lights at night and becomes a massive pleasure quarter for students and businessmen.

*Below* The city of Tokyo seen on a clear day. It has been the capital of Japan since 1868 when the Meiji government changed its name from Edo to Tokyo. Today it is the centre of administration, of the economy, and of culture and education. It has a population of over 11 million.

The impression that many people have of Tokyo is of a nightmarish jungle of concrete, neon, telephone wires, people, and more people. In the 1970s it was the world's largest city with a population of around ten million, and even though it has long since been surpassed by Mexico City and Cairo it remains a densely packed metropolis. Nevertheless, it has many admirers, one of whom has claimed that, 'in function and scale it is the equal of New York but without the slums, and in urban beauty it is the equal of Paris while exceeding it in energy and activity'. It is without a shadow of doubt a city of great energy and movement and one that encompasses a range of services and roles that many find intoxicating. But, of course, it has its slums, for example on the reclaimed land facing Tokyo Bay in the eastern part of the city; and what urban beauty Tokyo may have is extremely difficult to find even in the older parts.

Tokyo's attractions lie elsewhere, for example in the safety on the streets, day or night, that Japanese take for granted in all their cities. Tokyo may equal Los Angeles and London in size, but it has none of the violence and the rising crime rates, particularly for burglaries and rapes. There can be

few major cities safer for a woman walking alone at night than Tokyo and few where in some years the crime rate declines. An English reporter has claimed that 'the price of this freedom from crime is eternal vigilance that sometimes borders on prying that people in Britain might well resent' and has described Japan as 'the friendly neighbourhood police state'. Just what form does this 'eternal vigilance' take?

The role played by the *koban*, or police-box, in Japanese society is an important one to consider here. These are small police sub-stations, which in the cities are worked by police officers in shifts and are responsible for perhaps 300 or so households. In rural districts the *koban* are residential and responsible for a large number of households. The officers on duty spend several hours a day visiting and talking to the families and businesses on their 'beat', indeed they are required to do this at every home and business at least twice a year and to keep a book in which they record details of the family members, of any lodgers, and so on. The image that the police try to create of themselves, though it is one that has become a little tarnished in recent years, is one of neighbourly service, as this verse from the official police song shows:

> O we of the new day
> Filled with the love of gentle breeze
> Hold aloft the banner of freedom
> Beautiful, flowing
> Sacred, the duty of public peace
> Genial, drawing close, smiling, truthful
> Friend of the people.

Nobody is required to respond to the policeman's questioning when he drops in for a cup of tea, let alone to treat him as a friend, but most do, if

*Right* One of Tokyo's attractions is the safety of its streets. Here a young schoolgirl returns home alone with no fear for her safety.

*Opposite* An ultra-modern police box in Tokyo, which is well-known for its abstract design of an owl. This is an appropriate symbol of the quiet and watchful police. Japan is proud of its low crime rate and police boxes are found in most neighbourhoods at large street junctions. Each box is constantly manned and is responsible for a fairly small area.

*Above left* A police box in the Ginza, the most fashionable area of shops in Tokyo. At night the Ginza is a dazzling night spot with popular restaurants, bars and coffee shops lining the back alleys off the main street.

*Above right* Elsewhere in Japan replica policemen are placed at intervals along the road to remind motorists of the speed limit.

only to avoid getting on the wrong side of the law. As a result each police-box is very informed about its immediate neighbourhood. What sort of information is it that they are looking for? Lists of old people living alone, of people with criminal records or a history of mental illness, of people who work on night shifts and might therefore be unknowing witnesses of crimes committed at night, and so on. This information is derived both from the home visits that the policemen make and also from local neighbourhood groups, crime prevention associations, and even from overly zealous neighbours as the following illustrates: 'A woman come to me last week,' Sergeant Mizukami says, and said, 'My neighbour may have come into a lot of money lately, by the way their living style has changed. They've got a brand new car and the curtains are new and they've got a stereo set which they certainly didn't have before.' The sergeant says he filed the report with Chofu main station. 'Senior officers will decide if it is necessary to dispatch plain-clothes detectives to conduct a secret investigation.' This particular report smacks of jealousy but it is the store of often trivial information of this sort that is sifted through by policemen investigating serious crimes in the hope of finding unusual or suspicious patterns of behaviour.

Without the cooperation of the local population this kind of policing would clearly be impossible, so why do people cooperate? Some undoubtedly cooperate for negative reasons: not to do so is obviously to make yourself conspicuous in the eyes of the police. But, equally, many find the density of police presence in residential neighbourhoods reassuring. It does entail some loss of privacy, to be sure, but against that must be weighed the peace of mind that comes from knowing that your children are in no danger when they come home from school by themselves or play with their friends in the neighbourhood. There is no need for the precautions that are now becoming commonplace in Western cities: it is common to see six-year-old children travelling home from school by train or bus and then walking the rest of the way home by themselves.

Intimate policing of this kind is all very well in established residential urban districts and in rural areas, but it is proving difficult to operate in the large apartment complexes that have been constructed on the outskirts of many Japanese cities to overcome the housing shortage. The police have found that the residents of these complexes tend to be less cooperative and that they have much less to do with their neighbours than other suburban residents. They are much less likely to form voluntary neighbourhood crime prevention organizations and often have a much more highly developed sense of privacy, perhaps because of the cheek-by-jowl nature of apartment-block life. The routine of friendly home visits and informal contacts with the police is almost a different world, but the more formal policing of the apartment complexes seems set to spread as patterns of urban living change and juvenile crime increases.

Organized crime exists in Japan just as it does everywhere else in the world. Gangsters are called *yakuza* in Japanese, and it would be a mistake to see them as something like a Japanese mafia. Although it is undeniable that there are some similarities, the differences are much greater, for the yakuza are very much a product of Japanese society. It is, for example, difficult to imagine a building in New York rubbing shoulders with the Chrysler building but labelled 'Mafia Headquarters'. It is similarly difficult to imagine a local television news item reporting the return of a prominent gang leader from a vacation in Hawaii with shots of him driving away from the airport in a huge limousine, or even researchers interviewing mafia godfathers for information on the social significance of gangs. But the yakuza do put the names of their gangs on the front of the buildings that serve as gang headquarters, for they like to preserve a façade of respectability; one of the larger gangs even publishes a regular illustrated magazine for its members. They do occasionally appear on television returning from their summer holidays, and they even pay tax on their illegal earnings, though like everybody else they are allowed to make deductions for necessary expenses, including for example daily allowances for gangsters on intimidation duty. One such gangster did give an interview to a university researcher:

'When I visited the home of a gangster boss in Okayama, the boss and his immediate *kobun* (underling) came out to my car to greet me when I arrived (a favour usually reserved for only the most honoured guests in Japan), and then they formally escorted me to my car after the interview. Several of the gangsters stopped traffic so I could leave easily. While I was at his home, one of his underlings shined my shoes.'

Japanese gangsters may have better manners than the mafia, but what do they really do?

My first landlady in Kyoto had found herself in the clutches of the yakuza through borrowing money in order to keep up the large, decaying family house. She had no way of earning her own living; her elder brothers had wanted her to care for their ailing mother in her final illness and had therefore deliberately arranged no marriage for her; now they gave her as little to live on as they thought they could get away with. She was, in other words, just the right prey for the loan-sharks and the yakuza, for she was alone, too ignorant to realize that she had long since paid back all she owed, and frightened enough to pay up.

When short of money to hand over, her usual trick when the yakuza came was to hide in the parts of the house which had fallen down, or in the muddle of her bedroom. They always came in pairs and in the evening. She had to be quick enough to turn off the lights before they came into the house: otherwise they would know she was hiding somewhere.

One evening she was unlucky. They saw her in the hall turning off the lights and went after her. She put up a fight, first by shouting at them and then by racing into the back part of the long traditional house which my wife and I were renting. The first that I knew of what was happening was shouting and then the sound of several pairs of running feet (yes, the yakuza had remembered to take off their shoes, as is the Japanese custom, before entering the house to beat up the owner). The next thing I saw was my fortunately agile landlady leaping down the steps into our kitchen, where I was making some tea; she hopped over the rice cooker and came to a halt behind me. The stage was set for a stirring scene of defending the weak, but events suddenly took a bizarre turn. The two yakuza stopped at the entrance to the kitchen, smoothed their faces, bowed, handed over their visiting cards, and switched from abuse to polite language. Their cards gave not only their names but also their place of business, in other words gang affiliation, and their telephone numbers. They politely informed me that my landlady owed them some money, and asked me to hand her over so that they could beat her up for not paying. Once I refused, however, their language deteriorated and instead of soothing honorifics I got a stream of the most interesting Japanese abuse. But I had their names and they knew they were beaten. They slunk off home, with my landlady unwisely sauntering down the hall after them to shout a few bits of choice abuse as they put their shoes on. When I finally sat down the tea was cold, my thesis was behind schedule, but my Japanese vocabulary was infinitely richer.

Another time I was visiting a friend of mine who is a university professor. He wanted to sell his apartment to move to a larger one and he had been lucky enough, so he thought, to find a purchaser privately. Unfortunately, house conveyancing is another area which yakuza are interested in and one day when I happened to be visiting him a yakuza dropped in. What he wanted was the fee that he or somebody like him would normally have received if the sale had been handled by an estate agent in the usual way. He

*Opposite* As most businessmen keep a mirror-like shine on their black shoes, shoeshiners are plentiful in the business districts. The customer is reading about AIDS in his paper.

*Above left* A telephone sex-club. Boys join the club where girls telephone in. If the girls like the sound of the boys only then do they arrange a meeting.

*Above right* Late-night entertainment – the entrance to a live sex show. The posters describe it as a 'Love Clinic' and warn yakuza to keep away.

*Left* On a side street in Harajuku, the fashion centre for teenagers and the young at heart, a discarded mannequin is recycled into street art.

argued that there was a principle at stake. Since the sum was a matter of several thousand pounds, the professor refused even to entertain the idea of paying the money, until the yakuza changed the subject. He started talking about the dangers of the modern world and how easy it was for an accident to happen even, say, to a professor's son. Needless to say, he got his money.

The schemes used by the yakuza to gain their funds are various and currently growing more imaginative. Apart from their connections with loan-sharks and house conveyancing they also run protection rackets which bring them a steady income from amusement arcades, bars and similar establishments. There is money to be made from prostitution, drugs, illicit gambling, gun-running (because of Japan's strict laws on the possession of firearms), and pornography-smuggling, for magazines like *Playboy* fall foul of the Japanese law forbidding the appearance of pubic hair in illustrations. Some have found it profitable to buy shares in a number of major companies and use the opportunity to attend the annual shareholders' meetings to do a bit of useful extortion. They may simply threaten to disrupt the meeting, they may offer to prevent dissatisfied shareholders from putting their views across, or they may dig up some scandal concerning the company's

*Left* A busy city street on which a palm reader waits for customers. Those with the best reputations often have queues of waiting clients.

activities or better still the private lives of the directors and threaten to inform the meeting of what they know, but in any case they are usually paid off by the management. Yakuza are now dealing internationally, setting up laboratories in Taiwan and South Korea to make the amphetamines that they then smuggle to Japan, running massage-parlours for Japanese tourists in Hawaii, organizing the notorious 'sex tours' to South-East Asia or recruiting South-East Asian prostitutes to work in Japan on tourist visas.

Yakuza are reputed to be intensely patriotic and strongly right-wing in their views. They have even on occasion cooperated with the police and conservative politicians to control demonstrations and outbreaks of public disorder, the most famous occasion being the chaotic upheavals which preceded President Eisenhower's proposed visit to Japan in 1960 and which led to its cancellation. What is more, they claim to stand up for traditional values, such as loyalty, a sense of obligation, and the *oyabun-kobun* relationship. These two words mean something like 'boss' and 'follower' but their literal meaning is 'father role' and 'child role' and the relationships between the two are ostensibly the cement that holds yakuza gangs together.

'The yakuza I talked to insisted that this relationship was based not on fear but on respect. Should the oyabun die, the kobun must avenge him. This explains why last summer a young gangster called Marumi decided to swallow the ashes of his murdered boss and have a go at killing the leader of the rival gang.'

*Right* A girl hands out publicity for a sex shop to a likely looking customer in the entertainment or pleasure quarters of Tokyo.

*Left* This striking ultra-modern cylindrical building in Tokyo's Ginza houses many small businesses. East and West are alternately represented by European fashions: Kimono, a 'French Café', and a Japanese-style drinking place, on ascending floors of the same building.

*Below* Kabuki is one of Japan's most popular performing arts. The actors are always dressed in sumptuous kimonos, and wear the traditional white make-up. This type of drama originated in the seventeenth century. The plays contain much action, have elaborate sets and are performed using stylized dialogue with unique dances and music.

In many respects yakuza gangs have had something traditional, even exciting and certainly colourful about them. The yakuza film is an established genre in Japan, though not one that is much known in the West, and the standard line is to present the gang leader as a hero. But the image is wearing thin these days, partly because the involvement of the yakuza in the spread of drugs is now affecting a much larger proportion of the population. It is therefore becoming more and more common to use a less ambiguous word to describe the gangsters, *boryokudan*, which means 'violence groups'. Violence is, after all, what they purvey.

The yakuza have their origins in the gambling fraternities and outlaw groups of the Tokugawa period (1600-1868), which was also the age of growth for the Japanese city and of the development of such features of urban life as close neighbourly cooperation. The basis of this growth was the settlement of the samurai as bureaucrats in the castle-towns of their daimyo lords. To service this core population of samurai, merchants settled in the castle-towns in large numbers and provided the food, clothing, equipment and housing for the entire town. In Edo, now called Tokyo, which was little more than a village at the end of the sixteenth century, the samurai formed well over half the total population, for Edo was the seat of the shogun's government and all the daimyo had to maintain permanent residences there.

The rigid class system imposed by the Tokugawa shoguns was one that gave pride of place to the samurai and the lowest place of all to the merchants and artisans of the towns and cities. But by the eighteenth century the social order had been turned upside down by the economic relationships prevailing between the samurai and the 'townsmen', as the merchants and artisans were called. This anomalous situation was created by the disdainful refusal of the shogun's government, and of samurai in general, to concern themselves with economic matters. They maintained the fiction that Japan was still an agrarian society with a rice economy, but in practice it had transformed itself very rapidly in the course of the seventeenth century into a money economy. Samurai stipends were paid in rice but goods had to be purchased with hard cash, so the samurai had first to sell their rice on the open market. If the price was high they would benefit, but if it was low they could find themselves desperately short of money. The rice market was in the hands of the rice brokers and subject to all the market forces of supply and demand, with the result that a given rice income fluctuated wildly from year to year.

While the samurai, and many daimyo too, were increasingly finding themselves financially embarrassed, the townsmen were amassing fortunes, parading their wealth, and making it grow still further by making loans to hard-pressed samurai. Yodoya, one of the wealthiest, tried the patience of the government too far and in 1705 had most of his assets confiscated.

It was the prosperity of many of the merchant houses in Osaka and Kyoto that supported a burgeoning townsmen's culture. Edo was growing rapidly and its population was to reach one million in the eighteenth century, but it was still a new city at the beginning of the seventeenth century, and it was in the already established cities of Osaka and Kyoto in the west of Japan that the culture of the townsmen first grew to prominence. It was a culture based on the values of the merchant class and on the cultural heroes of the day. Its setting was either the merchant quarters or the pleasure quarters, which were the streets of prostitution and entertainment and which functioned as an outlet for the energies of a growing class that could find no political voice.

The iconoclastic products of the new merchant culture survived to acquire respectability in the nineteenth century, and even international fame. These included the kabuki theatre and the puppet theatre, both of which have now toured Europe and North America. There were new poetic forms such as the haiku, which is renowned as one of the shortest of all poetic forms and which several Western poets have experimented with in recent years. There was a new genre of fictional literature set in Osaka and Kyoto and written by townsmen for townsmen. And there were the 'floating world' prints, popular prints of courtesans, sumo wrestlers and actors, which were so admired by Monet and van Gogh. With his brother, Vincent van Gogh collected over 400 of them, some of which he painted copies of in oils. The culture of the townsmen was the antithesis of the samurai culture of Chinese learning, with the Noh theatre and swordsmanship, and its iconoclasm was apparent both in the popularity of parodies of the

*Opposite* The dressing room in a kabuki theatre. Here the male actors are preparing themselves for female roles. In the seventeenth century the government learned that actresses in kabuki plays were advertising themselves as prostitutes through the theatre. From that time no women have appeared on the kabuki stage.

124

The world Saikaku is describing here is one in which values have been changing rapidly and have begun to resemble twentieth-century sensibilities. Religious piety can be parodied and ridiculed in a way that would have been unthinkable a hundred years earlier, while the enjoyment of the pleasures of life have become an acceptable literary topic.

The age of Saikaku was also the age of Basho, the master of haiku poetry, and of Chikamatsu, the playwright often described as the Shakespeare of Japan. The surge of prosperity that gave the merchant class its confidence was then at its peak, but during the eighteenth century rising from rags to riches was no longer so easy. The established merchant houses had learned to protect their share of the market by developing guilds and by what we would call today restrictive practices.

What had started out as the vulgar culture of the townsmen in the seventeenth century became in the eighteenth the culture of all city dwellers, irrespective of class. Samurai were going to the kabuki theatre, albeit in disguise, they were writing popular novels, and they were visiting the courtesans in the pleasure quarters. They continued to have problems converting their rice incomes into cash and were frequently in debt. The shogun's government was not blind to the problems of the class it looked to for support but it did fail to perceive the realities of the commerical economy. It dealt with the problem of indebted samurai by unilaterally cancelling all debts from time to time, but this simply had the embarrassing effect of making it harder for needy samurai to secure the loans they required to live. And yet, at the same time, the merchants who had succeeded in making themselves wealthy were subject to no systematic taxation: unlike the strict agricultural taxes, urban taxes were levied on an unsystematic basis and there can be no doubt that the government neglected its fiscal opportunities.

By the early years of the nineteenth century the range of pleasures, diversions and entertainments offered by the cities was vast. They catered, of course, to all sorts of tastes. There were no museums or art galleries in the modern sense, but there were numerous exhibitions of calligraphy, painting, and poetry, and of horticultural specimens, medicinal herbs and even medical equipment. There were also exhibition booths, where the crowds could see, for example in 1674 a giant woman more than seven feet tall, in 1791 a parrot that could produce imitations of famous kabuki actors, and in 1821 a pair of camels. In effect Edo and the other major cities formed a mass society ruled by the tastes of the urban crowd. It was money that mattered, not rank or class, and there is more than a hint here of the mass society of modern Japan, which takes its pleasures without being unduly troubled by distinctions of class.

City life also had its dangers. The most terrifying was fire. In a city like Edo, where houses were made of wood and windows were paper-covered screens and where there were streets of tenement houses tightly packed together, fire was a constant risk and would spread very quickly once established. There were more than 90 major fires in Edo between 1600 and 1868, and some of them were catastrophic: the great fire of March 1657 destroyed half of the city and, when it had finally burned itself out after three days,

*Opposite* One of the dangers of life in the city was the risk of fire. In Edo the houses were made of wood and tightly packed together. The great fire in 1657 destroyed much of the city. Desperate people tried to escape with their possessions in mobile chests, but caused even more havoc in the crowded streets.

more than 100,000 had perished, either in the flames or from exposure during the snowstorm that enveloped the city afterwards. To Westerners who saw Edo in the 1850s and 1860s, the debris of previous fires was an awesome reminder of the dangers:

> It is impossible to ride through the streets of Yeddo without noticing one of the most striking and constant features of the city, large gaps where charred timber and rubbish mark the scene of the recent fire. It is very rare that the night passes without the fire-bell of the quarter ringing a fearful alarm and rousing all the neighbourhood.

The fire-bells were rung from towers set up throughout the city to give early warning of an approaching fire. A ban on thatched roofs in the city and the broadening of some main thoroughfares to act as firebreaks were of some help in preventing the spread of fires, but not if the wind was up. Each quarter had its fire-brigade, equipped with water pumps and hooks to pull off burning roofs, but many of the 'flowers of Edo', as the fires were called, were too much for them. All residents were conscious that their valuables were constantly at risk. The wealthy had storehouses with thick walls of plaster rather than wood which could resist all but the fiercest

In the nineteenth century bell towers were built so that local inhabitants could be warned of an approaching fire.

conflagrations, but the rest had only chests fitted with wheels. Belongings could be crammed into these at the last moment, but the difficulty of moving them in the congested streets cost many their lives. A Dutchman in Edo during the great fire of 1657 left a harrowing account of the panic:

> We all now realized that escape was our only choice. Servants and retainers hurried this way and that. By the time our senior Japanese staff had sealed the storehouse and organized our flight, I saw that the flames were but a pistol shot away from our door. With our realization of the gravity of the situation at about half past four, our senior Japanese bodyguard, with a long staff in hand, led us into the street with instructions to stay together at all costs. This was indeed almost impossible because of the crowds of panic-stricken refugees, many trying to carry away their belongings in big chests on four wheels. Those who were empty-handed climbed over the chests and packs, finding safe escape. We did likewise, as well as climbing over roofs in our race to outrun the insatiable flames that caught those wretched people who could not pass with their possessions. God save their souls.

Some major conflagrations were caused by earthquakes, rather than arson or accident. An overturned lamp or damage to a stove were enough to

Earthquakes can occur at any time in Japan and in a serious one there is great danger from fire. In Edo and the surrounding area there were earthquakes in 1783, 1860 and 1923. The illustration shows refugees fleeing from the earthquake in 1860. Today in Tokyo there are special evacuation areas in the event of a quake and most households keep an emergency supply of food and water.

Miyajima – one of the most famous beauty spots in Japan. Miyajima Island is designated a Special Historic Site and a Special Place of Scenic Beauty. The buildings of the Itsukushima Shrine are connected by corridors over the water. A shrine is entered through its torii or gates and at Miyajima these rise out of the sea forming a spectacular landmark.

set wooden houses ablaze. Minor earthquakes and tremors, many quite imperceptible without seismographic equipment, were a common part of life in Edo as they are in Tokyo today. But earthquakes at the top end of the Richter scale have also struck Edo and Tokyo and the surrounding area with grim regularity at intervals of around 70 years. The 1923 earthquake, the most recent, struck at noon, when in many houses fires were being kindled to prepare lunch. The strength of the initial tremor was sufficient to destroy many houses and buildings, but far more damage to both people and property was caused by the fires that soon spread throughout Tokyo and nearby Yokohama. More than 100,000 lost their lives, and more than 70 per cent of the inhabitants of the two cities lost their homes. Water supplies, telephones and transport were all badly hit, and public order broke

down completely: hundreds, and perhaps thousands, of Korean residents were killed by vigilante groups after rumours had circulated that Koreans had poisoned the water supply, and the military police took the opportunity also to kill a number of radical unionists and prominent anarchists.

Following the earthquakes of 1783, 1860 and 1923, there is widespread expectation of another before the end of the twentieth century. The city government has designated certain parks and open spaces as 'escape zones'; many families keep an emergency supply of food and medical dressings, and in certain parts of Tokyo there are annual earthquake drills during which local residents evacuate their houses and make their way to one of the 'escape zones'. A strong tremor can produce a flurry of activity in well-prepared families as parents, grandparents and children rush around to turn off the gas, open the door, place babies in the safest spot, and prepare for possible evacuation. It remains to be seen, however, if the buildings are as shock-proof and the contingency plans as thorough as they are supposed to be. These are serious worries, for Tokyo residents know only too well that the last major earthquake caused more deaths than any other civil disaster in the twentieth century.

It may be partly because of the very real dangers that the natural world holds for the inhabitants of the Japanese islands – floods and typhoons annually as well as earthquakes and fires – that the famous temple gardens display nature in a way that suggests it has been tamed and brought under control. Nevertheless, the Japanese have never shown any tendency to shun travel and exposure to the elements. On the contrary, since the Nara period (645-784) travel and the romance of place have been constant sources of poetic inspiration, and poetry has in turn acted as a stimulus to travel. Places such as Miyajima, traditionally considered one of the three finest scenic spots in Japan, are now overlayed with centuries of historical and literary associations that still call forth a response from travellers and inspire a constant flow of visitors.

In the Tokugawa period travel became a mass activity for the first time. Visiting Europeans in the seventeenth century expressed astonishment at the density of traffic on the roads and the constant movement of people throughout the country. The Tokaido highway linking Edo with Osaka was the most travelled route. It was served like the other major routes by frequent post-towns where accommodation could be had, new straw sandals could be bought, and horses could be hired for the next stage of the journey. The fastest travellers were the official couriers, who by dint of regular changes of horse and the priority they enjoyed at ferries could cover the 300 miles from Edo to Osaka in under four days. The slowest were the daimyo processions, consisting of the daimyo's great palanquin and a retinue of often hundreds of retainers travelling on foot. Since the daimyo were required to spend half the year in Edo and half in their domains, leaving their families behind in Edo as hostages, they made a permanent contribution both to the density of the traffic on the roads and to the economies of the post-towns they had to pass through.

Since the eighteenth century Japan's cities have grown at the expense of rural areas. Over three-quarters of the country is mountainous, and land

Working on the land. Since the 1950s farmers have been lured away to the large commercial and industrial cities and towns. Farmland near the cities has been developed and today much food is imported. However, families do continue to work the land. The main crops besides rice are tea, potatoes, tobacco, cereals and apples.

suitable for agriculture or urban development is consequently in short supply. Nevertheless, much of the nation's food does come from the land, and paddy-fields still cover most of the available agricultural land. Paddy farming demands intensive labour when transplanting the seedlings and fertilizing the land: the stubble has to be burned off each year and the ground fertilized, for unless this is done the land cannot be cultivated successively year after year. Thus the traditional Japanese extended-family system owes some of its characteristics to the nature of the task facing households dependent on rice cultivation: it is a cooperative and intensive grind and different in kind from European patterns of agriculture. Control of the water supply and the maintenance of some form of ditch and irrigation system are obviously essential as well for all members of a farming community, but the scale of this task requires cooperation on a community basis: it is too big even for individual families to cope with. Rice has inevitably dictated certain patterns of life in Japan, and the effects of this are still very much apparent today. Even now, when in many villages much of the basic work in the paddies is done by women while the men work as labourers or commute to office jobs, planting and harvesting and the care of the irrigation ditches are still done on a cooperative basis, with the

Azaleas bloom in spring as the paddy fields are worked and the rice seedlings are transplanted. It is back-breaking work as is the weeding of the paddies that takes place over the following couple of months. Today sprays are also used against disease and weeds.

participation of all the villagers in everything from discussions about health care to gathering in the rice.

In post-war Japan the rural workforce has been in decline as sons and daughters move to the cities for their further education and then choose to settle there, but this has been partly offset by the development of compact agricultural machinery that has made rice-farming much less of a labour-intensive operation than it used to be. And the commitment of successive governments to supporting the price of rice at an artificially high level has brought a measure of affluence to village communities which with new technologies has radically altered patterns of work and relaxation. But as we have seen this has not broken the bonds that tie families to the community and make them mutually dependent on each other. As Ronald Dore, one of the shrewdest observers of rural Japan, has put it: 'The lack of what in other societies might be valued as "privacy" is part of what it means to be a "member" of a community.' In many small towns and villages, for example, it is not uncommon to find that every house is fitted with a loudspeaker through which an early-morning call and local announcements are made. The volume can be turned down but the loudspeaker cannot be turned off. It is not compulsory to have these loudspeakers fitted, but in any community that has such a system the likelihood is that nobody will refuse. Why? There is an incentive in that the loudspeaker comes with a telephone on which local calls can be made for no charge, and doubtless there are some peer-group pressures at work as well, but the system is seen on balance to be a token of belonging to the local community rather than an invasion of privacy.

The *giri*-books kept by some villages are another indication of the importance attached to maintaining village relationships. *Giri* is the word for a sense of obligation or duty, and in any small farming community obligations are the stuff of life. Since many of the tasks associated with rice-farming were beyond the capabilities of any one family each was forced to rely on neighbours' help and an obligation incurred in that way would later have to be paid back in a roughly equal extent to maintain the equilibrium of social relationships. Wedding gifts, help with the construction of a house, and so on, all involve a sense of being obligated to community neighbours, and the giri-books are simply records of these obligations. Sometimes they stretch back 80 years, but, however old, they summarize the ties that make a village a community rather than just a collection of houses.

The flow of younger villagers to the towns and cities, however, has raised questions about the survival of village communities. For the men it has

Gathering in the rice straw once the rice is harvested. When the plants are ripe the water supply to the paddies is cut off and the harvest begins. Today combine harvesters are used and these are shared by all the farms in the area.

been a question of jobs and particularly jobs that could become careers and involve less of the back-breaking work that rice-farming required. For the women it has also been a matter of avoiding the farming work that would often fall on their shoulders, and also of finding a husband with a salary to his name rather than just a few fields. In spite of these pressures leading to the depopulation of farming villages, Ronald Dore found in the village he studied, Shinohata, that a surprising number of eldest sons had followed tradition in giving up their city jobs and returning home to the country to take over the role of head of the family and maintain the family home. There are also signs that the one-way flow of the young to the cities may be coming to an end, and the government has in recent years been trying to encourage a measure of decentralization away from the conurbations of Tokyo and Osaka.

The main element of this new focus on regional development is the so-called 'technopolis project'. The project has been developed by the Ministry of International Trade and Industry (MITI) and the objective is to establish new industries based on advanced technologies, such as automation systems and biotechnology, in hitherto industrially underdeveloped parts of the Japanese islands. The reasoning behind the project is that younger

Mechanization has made agriculture easier – here a farmer transplants his rice seedlings with the help of an automatic machine. The seedlings are carried in the tray at the back of the machine.

There are still many small towns and villages in modern Japan. The pull of the big city is strong and many of the young leave the rural communities. Often these days it is left to the women to work the land while their husbands go off to an office job.

engineers and scientists from regional universities and research centres are no longer as keen as their predecessors to congregate in Tokyo or Osaka. The old castle-town of Kumamoto on Kyushu, which is the home of a vast semiconductor factory, is the first of the areas selected by MITI to be transforming itself into a technopolis and it has a large potential pool of engineers to draw upon. 'In 1984, of a total of 1,339 science and technology graduates 1,011 were forced to leave Kumamoto to find jobs. A survey, taken at the beginning of last year, of engineers from Kumamoto but working outside the prefecture, showed that half would like to return if a suitable job was available.' The introduction to Kumamoto of industries and research institutes at the forefront of advanced technology seems so far to have had a beneficial effect in stimulating technological development in existing local industries and thereby increasing local employment opportunities. Companies which used to produce wheelbarrows or wooden shoes have transformed themselves into much larger enterprises which now assemble semiconductors and have grown to many times their original size. In this area at least an answer has been found to the problem of rural depopulation, but it has been found not by market forces as such but by forward planning and encouragement on the part of both central and local government, an option that is ideologically unacceptable in several Western countries at the moment.

This fisherman is using a wooden box fitted with a glass bottom to search out schools of fish. The Japanese enjoy fish and seafood which play an important part in their diet.

There is one predominantly urban problem that no amount of government planning has yet been able to resolve and that many Japanese would be upset to find in a book such as this. It is the problem of minorities and discrimination. It is a problem that local government is keenly aware of, to the extent of urging citizens on local radio stations to help put an end to discrimination and resolve what is euphemistically called the 'assimilation problem'. This coy phrase is the code word for the problem of the *burakumin*, a minority within Japan of people who are ethnically Japanese but nevertheless discriminated against.

The origins of the burakumin lie in the outcast groups who filled the important function of carrying out jobs which were essential but, under the influence of Buddhism and particularly the Buddhist prohibition on the taking of life, considered to be polluting. They had a monopoly of such jobs as the slaughter of animals, the tanning of leather and the business of public executions, and it was their monopoly that gave them economic security right up to the end of the nineteenth century. At this stage, they became known as 'new citizens', a name that replaced the traditional term *eta*, which is written with Chinese characters signifying 'much filth'. But there has been a tendency for each new euphemism to acquire pejorative overtones and the word burakumin has itself acquired connotations that make its use a delicate matter.

A temple path in autumn

When in 1871 the burakumin had their officially inferior status cancelled, they lost their monopolies, and for legal purposes they became just as other Japanese. Ending the discrimination, however, was another matter. The emancipation edict itself proved unpopular in villages close to burakumin communities and there were a number of attacks on burakumin in the 1870s. In 1880 a booklet issued by the Ministry of Justice described them as 'the lowest of all people, almost resembling animals'. The persistent discrimination and the psychological strain, for burakumin trying to pass as 'ordinary' Japanese, of trying to conceal their origins was given dramatic expression in 1906 in a novel by Shimazaki Toson called *The Broken Commandment*. The hero of this novel, Ushimatsu, is himself a burakumin, but one who is passing as an ordinary Japanese and teaching in a country school. He is torn between his loyalty to his father's commandment that he should never reveal the secret of his birth and his desire to free himself from the psychological prison his obedience has placed him in. At the end of the book he makes his 'confession' to the children in his class, fully aware that it will cost him not only his job but also his hard-won social respectability:

> You will feel disgust and loathing for me now that I have told you what I am. But though I was born so low myself, I have done my best each day to teach you only what is right and true. Please remember this, and forgive me if you can for having kept the truth from you till today. . . . When you get home, tell your parents what I have said. Tell them that I confessed today, asking your forgiveness . . . I am an eta, an outcast, an unclean being!

The novel ends with Ushimatsu preparing to start a new life in Texas, which may seem a miraculous reversal of his fortunes and absurd as an ending. In reality, however, emigration was an option considered by many burakumin and acted upon by some.

The first of the many national movements organized by the burakumin for the improvement of their lot and their social emancipation was formed in 1903, and there are still many active today. The main areas of discrimination they are trying to fight are employment and marriage. There can be no doubt that a burakumin labours under a severe handicap when applying for jobs or seeking to marry. It is not that they are facially or in any other way physically distinguishable from other Japanese. But their home addresses give them away, for the burakumin communities are still sharply defined geographical areas; the situation is no better for those living out of these communities, for the use of detectives to check up on the background of prospective employees or marriage partners is not uncommon.

In spite of the official exhortations to refrain from practicing discrimination of any sort, the problem remains a pressing one for the burakumin and one which shows no sign of nearing a solution. Prejudices die hard, but this is not a uniquely Japanese problem. It is undeniable that the burakumin are better off in economic terms than the Australian aboriginals or minority groups in Britain and the United States, and less likely to be the victims of community violence. On the other hand, the poignancy of the situation for the burakumin is that, though they are not a racial minority, they are excluded from what is still a remarkably homogeneous society.

## CHAPTER SIX

# Domestic and Social Life

*Left* In Japanese towns there are now many blocks of apartments. Many were built to alleviate the chronic housing shortage after World War II. So many people live in the cities that space is restricted and expensive.

*Below* On 15 November Japanese families take their children to the Seven-Five-Three Festival at the Meiji Shrine in Tokyo. This is a traditional Shinto festival, much enjoyed by families.

Many foreign tourists in Japan are curious about Japanese domestic life and in response to their curiosity local tourist offices have instituted home-visit programmes which at least give tourists a glimpse of the inside of a Japanese home. Interesting though these may be, they are no way to gain an understanding of domestic routines and they commonly leave many questions unanswered.

There is, of course, no average Japanese family, but probably the most common pattern in the cities now is a household consisting of just parents and children, usually two. It is now much less common than it used to be to have grandparents living at home, and very rare indeed to have a live-in maid, although not unknown. The family home might be a detached house, which most aspire to and would opt for even at the expense of a longer journey to work, or it might be an apartment, in which case living room might be much reduced but commuting distances shorter.

*Above* Children start school at 8.30 a.m. and finish at 4.30 p.m. The schoolchildren here carry their regulation satchels on their backs – there is homework to be done each evening.

*Opposite* Often the same rooms are used for both living and sleeping with bedding stored away during the day and brought out at night. Mattresses called *futon* are laid out on the floor with a quilt used on top. In the morning the futon are aired on the balconies.

Whether apartment or detached house, there would be less space than most Westerners are used to. It is this that has given rise to the 'rabbit-hutch' view of Japanese life, but this can only be said to be an example of Western cultural arrogance. Precisely because space is at such a premium in Japanese homes, it has always been used economically and to great effect in a way that very few Western visitors have a chance to see for themselves. In smaller homes, for example, the main room in which visitors are entertained is transformed at night into the bedroom, as *futon* (mattresses) are laid out on the floor. One of the main morning rituals is the task of folding the *futon* up again and either putting them away in cupboards or airing them in the sun on the balcony. The entrance hall or *genkan* is a traditional feature of many homes, and here members of the family change from shoes into slippers and spare pairs are kept for visitors. Nobody walks on the floor of Japanese homes with shoes on.

For the Japanese the concept of private space is a relatively new one and the very word for 'privacy' is the English word pronounced in Japanese fashion. Until recently the need for private space within the home has been less than is now common in the individualistic West, though the exam pressures on teenagers have forced some changes in patterns of living, and now most have their own bedrooms. Beds have become more popular, partly as a status symbol and partly because they are more suited to the Western styles of detached house that are now much in demand.

Car ownership in Japan is now widespread and so large apartment blocks and detached houses automatically include spaces for parking cars. Those living in older houses or smaller apartment blocks have to find a permanent (and legal) place to park a car before they can obtain a licence that will enable them to drive it on the roads. This usually means a space in a neighbourhood parking lot for which a monthly fee is charged.

Since unemployment is still below five per cent, the chances are that the father goes out to work. In the largest cities that may involve a journey of about an hour by bus and train, and sometimes even as much as two hours each way. Since commuting is a fact of life for the majority of Japanese families, advertisements for new houses and apartments customarily give high prominence to transportation details: 'Seven minutes by foot from Tanabe station, 40 minutes by express train from Osaka'. Even if the working week is shifting from six days to five, the working day is rarely of the nine-to-five variety. Work is not taken home and overtime is quite common, so too is after-hours socializing with fellow employees, friends, contacts in other organizations, customers, and so on. Here the dividing line between 'work' and 'leisure' begins to break down. At any rate, the father may return at, say, 10 o'clock at night several times a week, particularly if he is ambitious or has a large circle of friends. Many might prefer to spend more time at home but business entertainment plays a vital role in maintaining the face-to-face contacts that cement business relationships. He will be able to charge

Many Japanese ride bicycles and there are often specially designated bicycle lanes in the towns. Shown here is a bicycle parking lot.

expenses of course, but there will be other expenses he will have to meet himself. Many companies, for example, circulate a weekly or monthly newsletter which lists, apart from other things, staff who have lost a member of their family through death. Colleagues and superiors, as well as friends, are expected to contribute to the heavy expenses associated with funerals in Japan. These are invariably Buddhist and cremation is the normal custom in Japan.

If the mother works her role will probably be clerical rather than executive. The family shopping is her responsibility. There are more shops per head of population in Japan than anywhere else in the world, so there is almost certain to be a good variety within the immediate vicinity of the family home, including both a supermarket and various shops selling fresh produce – vegetables, fruit, fish, meat, pickles. Few people shopping for food take lists with them, and daily shopping tends to be more common than the trip in a car to a large supermarket once a week. Local shops will often stay open late and, like major department stores and other city shops, they close one day a week but not on Sundays. For larger items that have been purchased, delivery is not only free within a radius of several miles but is often carried out the same day.

The evening meal is often decided by the freshest ingredients available. But whether it consists of meat or fish, it will always include a bowl of rice, usually eaten at the end of a meal with some pickled vegetables.

The rush hour. Commuting is part of most people's lives in Japan. In the large cities this can mean a journey of an hour by bus or train, sometimes longer, to their work. Many men are required to meet with colleagues and business associates after work and do not return home until late evening.

Rice, in one form or another, has worked its way into most corners of Japanese life. It is used to make rice gruel, or rice wine (*sake*). Rice straw provides many of the necessities of life: mats for homes, ropes, sacks and wrappers of various kinds, and the sacred rope hung in Shinto shrines as an expression of the community's dependence on rice. Straw ash has its uses too, as a bed for the coal in a charcoal brazier or as an ingredient of pottery glazes. Rice bran is used to pickle vegetables and until the nineteenth century a woman would use a small bag of rice bran as a kind of scrubbing brush to clean her face. Rice is also turned into a paste or starch used to

A sophisticated pedestrian crossing in the fashionable shopping area known as the Ginza in Tokyo. All the traffic is halted and pedestrians can then cross in any direction. There are more shops per head in Japan than anywhere else in the world.

stiffen ceremonial clothing, to glue paper windows in place, and to resist dyes so that patterns can be created on fabrics. Rice can also be pounded to make rice cakes which are a feature of New Year celebrations.

Today in a normal household weekday evenings are usually busy. For children, even at elementary school, there is usually a fair amount of home-work to get through, and for older children there may also be several hours at a crammer, or perhaps a ballet school or something similar. In the winter many families still use a *kotatsu* throughout the evening. A kotatsu is a square table with truncated legs and an electric heating-bulb attached to

*Below right* Railway waitresses sell snacks on express trains but here they pause for some food themselves. They are eating a picnic known as a *bento*. Such a snack is eaten with chopsticks and usually consists of rice with fish and vegetables, and soy sauce.

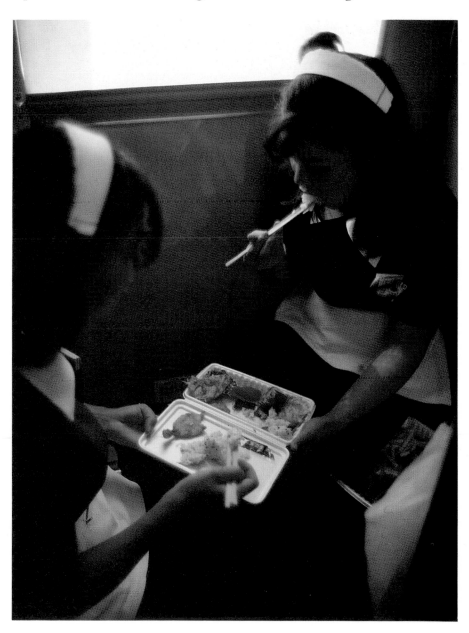

*Above* Bamboo rollers airing on a bicycle

*Opposite* Bathers in a hot-spring pool. Bathing is a ritual in Japan and it is just as much a way of relaxing and mixing socially as getting clean. After washing with soap outside the bath you soak yourself in the waters. At home the family will bathe together before having supper.

the underside: the table is covered with a blanket that hangs down on to the floor on all sides and on top of the blanket goes a flat table-top surface which can serve as dinner-table, desk, card-table or whatever. In older houses the kotatsu is fitted over a specially made depression in the floor which allows people to sit on the edge with their legs hanging down, but in modern apartments and new houses people sit around the kotatsu, with the blanket on their laps, and find room for their legs underneath. It is a cosy way to spend an evening, even if each member of the family is busy with something different. But Western-style patterns of life are popular too, and some families will sit in chairs and spend the evening reading or watching television. There are many channels to choose from and a variety of programmes from soap operas to quiz programmes and samurai drama.

The evening will always include one element that owes nothing to Western influence, the invigorating pleasures of a deep Japanese bath. The bathroom may be small and it may have no outside window, but it will always have a space in which to wash and rinse off and a deep tub in which to soak.

A nineteenth-century photograph of prostitutes bathing together

All the washing is done outside the tub, so the same hot water can be used by the whole family; if it cools down it can easily be reheated, for most baths have a reheating device. Japanese baths are at their best in the many *onsen*, or resorts, to be found throughout the Japanese islands. They offer large pools to bathe in, and often outdoor rock pools with natural hot water. In many *onsen* the waters have medicinal properties, but it is more common now to visit them for the sheer relaxation afforded by the baths.

Domestic and urban life have many advantages for the Japanese that are all but invisible to the Western visitor. The urban sprawl that all visitors see from the Bullet Train windows may look unattractive but it is now arguably the most successful urban society in the world. A businessman returning home late at night can rely on an efficient and reliable public transport system that is without equal. If he wants to buy anything from a bottle of whisky to a book he can do so from an automatic vending machine in his neighbourhood, which he can be sure will not have been vandalized. He can walk along deserted streets at night in the certainty that he will not be accosted or robbed. Most important of all, perhaps, he rests safe in the knowledge that his family is an integral part of a supportive local community; in case of need, neighbours can always be relied upon to lend a

A hot sand bath in Beppu. The spa town of Beppu is situated on the east coast of Kyushu, the southernmost island of Japan. The town, which is surrounded by volcanic mountains, has many hot-water baths and sand baths and it is also famous for its boiling mud ponds.

hand with anything from a wedding or funeral to sharing out a box of fruit sent by a cousin in the country. In a sense, the twentieth-century Japanese city has allowed many more of the values of village life to survive than have Western cities, and this is a major achievement that deserves to be more widely known in the West.

An image that is widely known in the West is that of the submissive, down-trodden Japanese woman. Like so many images of Japan this is an exaggeration although it also contains some elements of truth. What is certain is that the position of women in Japan has undergone enormous changes in the last 100 years and is still in a state of flux.

The first diplomatic mission sent by the Meiji government to the West, the Iwakura mission of 1872, included five young girls who spoke not a word of English. They were expected to stay with American families, be educated in America, and return to Japan as models of a new educated womanhood based on Western women. It was a revolutionary step and barely imaginable even a decade earlier.

For a millenium the position of women in Japanese society had been subject to the Buddhist teaching that women were inherently inferior and impure beings. This did not prevent them either from becoming nuns or

A Buddhist funeral service. The funeral ceremony is a Buddhist rite in Japan. Cremation and not burial is carried out and most families have elaborate gravestones erected in the cemeteries. Bosses and colleagues are expected to contribute to the heavy expenses associated with funerals.

from participating in pilgrimages, but it did mean that they were barred from certain sacred places, especially holy mountains, and that in some sects of Buddhism they were required to be reborn as men before they could enjoy the prospect of salvation. During the Tokugawa period (1600-1868) the teaching of Confucian moralists was that the duty of women was obedience throughout their lives, first to their fathers, then to their husbands and finally to their sons. Women could be divorced for trivial reasons such as garrulousness as well as for infertility, while they could only initiate a divorce if a husband had committed a serious crime or if they managed to gain sanctuary in a 'divorce temple'. Similarly, adultery by women could be, and often was in the seventeenth century, punished by death, but this did not apply to husbands' liaisons with courtesans or their concubines.

Two of the five girls who went to America in 1872 were Yamakawa Sutematsu, who was 12 years old at the time, and Tsuda Umeko, who was six. Yamakawa returned after she had completed a university education, and Tsuda returned after 10 years. Both were to all intents and purposes American girls when they returned. They wrote in their letters to American friends of the difficulties they experienced on returning to Japan and the

At Happo-en, a famous wedding hall and garden in Tokyo where as many as 40 couples are married a day. The couple on the left-hand side have opted for traditional dress and the groom will never again wear his formal Japanese dress. Almost one-half of all marriages in Japan are arranged. There is no question of forced marriage although there may naturally be some parental pressure. Wedding services are normally conducted as Shinto rituals.

sense of disappointment at the limited possibilities that were open to them. The government had met the costs of the experiment in sending them to America in the first place, but failed to find them roles once they were back in Japan. Yamakawa became the second wife of General Oyama, one of the founding fathers of the Japanese army, and could only satisfy her ambitions in voluntary administrative work for the Red Cross in Japan. Tsuda also had difficulties creating a role for herself, but she determined early in life not to marry and she refused the offer of a position at court as an interpreter. She returned to America for three years in 1889 to undertake some advanced studies in biology at Bryn Mawr College and later in 1900 founded the famous women's college in Tokyo that still bears her name, Tsuda College.

Tsuda found the situation for women distressingly different from what she had become accustomed to in America. To be born a Japanese woman, she felt, was to face a pitiable existence:

She is not often loved, often a plaything, oftener like a servant, but little educated. She believes herself perfectly happy, if she has a house, a husband and children. Every little girl in America ought to thank God for her lot.

In 1888 Tsuda and Yamakawa invited an American girl, Alice Bacon, to visit them in Japan. She had known them both well during their stay in the United States and after her visit wrote a book, entitled *Japanese Girls and Women*, which she dedicated to Yamakawa 'in the name of our girlhood's friendship, unchanged and unshaken by the changes and separations of our maturer years'. She paid tribute in it too to the help that Tsuda had been able to give her, and in 1900 she came to Japan a second time, on this occasion to help Tsuda establish her college.

In 1889 Alice Bacon attended the ceremonies marking the promulgation of the new Constitution:

> Upon this occasion, for the first time, the Emperor and Empress rode in the same coach, and it is really a great step up, so far as the women of the country are concerned. The theory hitherto has been that the Emperor is too far above his wife in dignity to appear in public with her in the same carriage, but yesterday, by riding with her, he recognized the fact that his own wife is raised by her marriage to his own social level. It is a formal adoption of the Western idea in regard to the position of the wife.

It was true that the Emperor Meiji, and his ministers, endeavoured to set an example of modernity and European manners in their marriages, and that the enthusiasm for Europe and America in the 1870s spread to the question of the role of women in the new Japan. In some circles, at least, there was a surge of ambition and optimism. It was hoped that the new Constitution would give women the vote, women's magazines devoted to literary, educational and political issues were founded, and novels that concentrated too much on the male perspectives of Meiji Japan came under criticism. But the Constitution promulgated in 1889 dashed any hopes that women might have the opportunity to vote, as it provided only for a limited male franchise. The franchise was only extended to women in Japan after World War II, partly at the urging of the American occupation forces and partly as a result of the campaigning of women's groups before the war.

Many of Alice Bacon's observations relate to women and marriage, for reasons that she makes clear in this passage, which at the same time can serve to emphasize how unusual Tsuda was in her determination not to marry.

> The alternative of perpetual spinsterhood is never considered, either by herself or by her parents. Marriage is as much a matter of course in a woman's life as death, and is no more to be avoided. This being the case, our young woman has only as much liberty of choice accorded to her as is likely to provide against a great amount of unhappiness in her married life. If she positively dislikes the man who is submitted to her for inspection, she is seldom forced to marry him, but no more cordial feeling than simple toleration is expected of her before marriage.

This passage encapsulates the distaste that the idea of arranged marriages arouses in the West. It is, of course, true that such marriages were once common in Europe, but why, it is asked, should they still be common in a Japan that in so many other respects seems to have become so Westernized? The kind of arranged marriage described by Alice Bacon, however, is very much a thing of the past.

Japanese teenagers would prefer to marry for love like their Western counterparts but in practice they expect to choose a partner in consultation with their parents. Teenagers are very fashion-conscious and pay great attention to their dress.

In response to surveys, Japanese teenagers overwhelmingly express a preference for 'love matches' but expect in practice to marry someone at least in part chosen in consultation with their parents. In many cases the business of arranging marriages is much akin to the work of marriage bureaux and dating agencies in Western countries. The parents, friends and business associates might circulate a folder containing photographs, a curriculum vitae and details such as hobbies and interests until it attracts the attention of a possible partner. Then it is a matter of arranging a meeting to see what they think of each other; if nothing comes of it then that is the end of the matter. Many will come to the defence of this contemporary form of the arranged marriage. Some argue that 'arranged marriages start out cold and get hot, whereas love matches start out hot and grow cold'. Others remain convinced that 'marriage partners chosen by one's parents in consultation with respected, experienced go-betweens, have greater chance of success'. Doubtless there are family pressures brought to bear in some cases, as of course there are in all countries, but for the most part arranged marriages in Japan, which now still account for roughly half of all marriages, have in fact moved away from the coercive model to the marriage-bureau model.

Another issue which caught Alice Bacon's attention was prostitution, and her comments were rather more perceptive than most:

> Japanese public opinion, though recognizing the evil as a great one, does not look upon the professional prostitute with the loathing which she inspires in Christian countries. The reason for this lies, not solely in the lower moral standards although it is true that sins of this character are regarded much more leniently in Japan than in England or America. The reason lies very largely in the fact that these women are seldom free agents. Many of them are virtually slaves, sold in childhood to the keepers of the houses in which they work, and trained for the life which is the only one they have ever known.

The licensed quarters and their courtesans had attracted the interest of the prurient, the moralistic and the licentious from the 1850s, when Westerners first began to reside in Japan. Prostitution first acquired political overtones in 1872 when a Peruvian steamer docked at Yokohama with several hundred Chinese coolies aboard who had been taken to be sold as slave labour. When ordered to release them, the resourceful captain accused the Japanese of hypocrisy, on the ground that the courtesans were slaves too. The Japanese judge argued that exporting slaves was a different matter altogether, but he was evidently struck by the captain's point, for he urged the government to liberate the courtesans from their bondage.

Later that year the first tentative laws were issued banning public prostitution, and as such they were early by international standards. In England, for example, the Public Prostitution Law was only repealed in 1886. However, new laws issued the following year instituted a system of private contractual arrangements between courtesans and the brothel managers, thus effectively shelving the legislation that had been issued only the previous year. But there was a growing movement for the abolition of prostitution, which was led by the rising numbers of Japanese Christians but which also enjoyed the support of a number of leading intellectuals.

The Salvation Army, which began activities in Tokyo in 1895, was also involved in the campaign to end prostitution and in giving help to girls who ran away from the brothels to which they had been indentured. It also set up a branch in Manchuria, where large numbers of Japanese prostitutes went after the Russo-Japanese War to cater to Japanese colonists. By 1914 there were 16,000 Japanese prostitutes in China, and more in several other countries with substantial Japanese communities, including the United States. Japanese diplomatic representatives overseas were as a result beginning to worry about the reputation of Japan and the possibility of growing anti-Japanese feeling. But the anti-prostitution lobby faced obstacles, especially the close links between police and brothel managers. In 1911, for example, a policeman who wrote an article exposing his colleagues' failure to ensure that the managers behaved legally was dismissed for his pains. Another obstacle was the underlying economic problems. The disastrous harvest of 1934, for example, left many families with a choice between starvation or selling a daughter into prostitution.

Alice Bacon's overall view of the position of women at the end of the nineteenth century was not encouraging:

*Opposite* A woman farm-worker in normal working clothes. Before World War II many working women in rural areas had more freedom than women from the higher classes. Their lives were busier and they contributed much to the family income.

There seems no doubt at all that among the peasantry of Japan one finds the women who have the most freedom and independence. Their lives are fuller and happier than those of the women of the higher classes, for they are themselves bread-winners, contributing an important part of the family revenue, and they are obeyed and respected accordingly. The Japanese lady, at her marriage, lays aside her independent existence to become the subordinate and servant of her husband and parents-in-law, and her face, as the years go by, shows how much she has given up, how completely she has sacrificed herself to those about her.

There can be no doubt that the position of women in Japanese society today is immeasurably better than it was before World War II. The new Japanese Constitution, enacted in 1946 under the aegis of the occupation authorities, outlawed discrimination on the basis of sex as well as on the basis of creed, race, social status or family origin. In theory, Japanese men and women have enjoyed equal rights, but some anomalies have remained. A number of the civil service entrance examinations were not open to women, for example, and women marrying foreigners did not have the right to pass their nationality on to their children. In April 1986, however, an Equal Opportunity Employment Bill came into effect which rectified these anomalies and brought Japanese law into line with the United Nations Convention on eliminating discrimination against women, signed by Japan in 1980. Nevertheless, although this new law encourages employers to conform to the principles of equal rights and opportunities, it embodies no sanctions to be used against recalcitrant companies.

How one views the lot of Japanese women today depends to some extent on one's standards and perspectives. Are they 'strictly bound by the rule of segregation and the division of labour, confined to domestic drudgery, and pitiably deprived in status, power and opportunities'? Or is it the case that the Japanese housewife chooses to stay at home, that she 'holds and exercises dictatorial power over the household affairs and enjoys unlimited autonomy'? These two points of view contradict each other, though both contain elements of truth; reconciling them is not easy.

It is possible to apply various yardsticks, such as access to education, employment, the political process and birth-control, to the position of Japanese women in order to see how they fare by comparison with women in other countries. As far as education is concerned, for example, they fare relatively well. More girls than boys now stay on at school beyond the school-leaving age. The participation of girls in higher education has also been rising steadily and now roughly one-third of all students in higher education are women. On the other hand, it can be objected that the majority of women students are enrolled in two-year junior colleges rather than the four-year regular universities, that they are still a small, albeit growing, presence in the most prestigious national universities, and that they tend to congregate in the humanities, nursing and home economics courses.

Employment, however, is a more complex issue. It is sometimes claimed that Japan's low unemployment figures – though they are rising now – have been achieved at the cost of employment opportunities for women, but this does not bear close examination. Some 15 million Japanese women have jobs now, and they constitute about 40 per cent of the work-force; more than half of them are married. However, their rewards at work are low, standing on average at barely half the average male wages. Opportunites to embark on a career or enter management are limited. The recent appoint-ments of women to prominent positions in the judiciary and academia and of a woman to the head of the Japan Socialist Party indicate that the highest positions are not completely closed to women, but the overall percentages of women in the professions are low, in most cases at less than 10 per cent.

As for political rights, the revision of the Electoral Law in 1945 gave women the right to vote and to stand for the Diet, Japan's parliament. Over 20 million Japanese women, nearly 70 per cent of those eligible, voted in

Doi Takako, the present leader of the Japan Socialist Party. She is the first woman to head a political party in Japan. Although the top positions in politics, industry and commerce are not closed to women the number employed in the professions is still low.

Dressed to impress. Children are greatly respected in Japan hence the several festivals held in their honour.

the first election after the war in 1946, and the participation of women in the voting process now exceeds that of men. On the other hand, the number of women in the Diet remains small: there were 39 after the 1946 election, but now there are just 27 women in a Diet with 759 members. In this respect, of course, Japan differs little from other countries.

For most of the pre-war period the government was opposed to any form of birth-control because of the threat it was thought to pose to the family and the nation. Condoms were, however, openly on sale to troops to prevent the spread of venereal disease. In 1922 the American birth-control compaigner Margaret Sanger visited Japan in spite of being refused a visa. Her visit gave the Japanese birth-control movement much greater impetus and influence than before. One of the leaders of this movement found herself bitterly attacked on the ground that she ought to be 'urging my sex to bear as many soldiers – noble patriots – as they possibly could'. In 1937 as the war in China was increasing demands for soldiery, the birth-control movement was suppressed and there was a total ban on all forms of birth-control. In contemporary Japan, however, the main form of contraception is the condom, which is frequently sold by door-to-door saleswomen, who come equipped with a large range of samples and whose sales patter would surprise Westerners with stereotyped ideas of the demure Japanese housewife. The pill has never been legally available, ostensibly for medical reasons: cynics have argued that the real reason is that there is more money to be made out of abortions than out of the pill.

Few American or British women would willingly choose to change places with a Japanese woman: the adjustments they would have to make would be considerable, as some non-Japanese women who have married Japanese men have found. However, Japanese women do not necessarily see things in quite the same way. This is illustrated by the following quote from a woman who graduated in the States and decided to return to Tokyo where she found a job and married.

> My husband was running a small family company, and if I had continued to work, the neighbourhood would have assumed that the business was not going well, so I left my job and started to work for my husband at home. My American friends would look at my small house and conclude that the quality of life would have been better in the States. But I can't agree with that. I'm working for something I want to succeed. I have my family near me, and I have a stake in this society.

Japanese perceptions are not necessarily the same as those common in the West. This is certainly true of perceptions of space, work and leisure: whether it is true of sexual roles too is at least debatable.

One of the tasks that is commonly entrusted to women in Japan is the management of their children's education: those who are most energetic in pursuit of this goal have acquired the sobriquet, 'education mummies', which is not intended as a compliment. Education is a problem. The fate awaiting almost every child is the notorious 'examination hell', which determines which university he or she will graduate from, a factor that will in turn be of crucial importance in the rat-race for the best jobs. Many parents conclude

A Middle School girl rides home from school – she is wearing a helmet for safety. The education system is divided into five stages: nursery (3-6), primary (6-12), middle (12-15), high (15-18), followed by a 4-year degree course at university.

that they have no choice in the matter and with many misgivings they commit their children to outside tutors and crammers in addition to their school work even before they are 12 years old. There are few opportunities for 'late developers'.

It is taken for granted that the goal is university, for without a degree there is virtually no chance of a secure career. The problem is which university, for the pecking-order of the universities in Japan, both private and public, is well-known. The high-flying grades of the bureaucracy and the large corporations recruit from the university elite, most prominent among which is Tokyo University. The most important stage of the whole process of education is the university entrance exam: it is of far more importance, in fact, to have graduated from the right university than to have left with a good degree.

A consequence of this is increased pressure at earlier stages of the education system. Some high schools are highly sought after because they have a good record for university entrants, but in order to pass the entrance exams for these schools it is necessary to find a good junior high school. Amid such competition, *juku*, or crammers, and private tutoring are normal. The latter is not a new phenomenon and for many generations of university students outside tutoring has been the source of essential funds to meet their living expenses. Crammers, however, are a relatively new phenomenon. It is estimated that 25 per cent of all schoolchildren under 12, and 50 per cent of those aged between 12 and 15, attend a private crammer in the evenings after school or on Sundays, and the crammer business has become a multi-million-pound industry.

The nature of university entrance examinations and the educational orientation they foster has come under increasing criticism. The entrance examinations, which take place without any interviews, consist solely of multiple-choice questions. Whatever the merits or demerits of the examination system itself, it has certainly familiarized generations of schoolchildren with an ethos of pressurized and competitive work that has effectively been put to use during Japan's phenomenal economic growth. For defenders of the present system the fact that it has made an important contribution to industry in this way is something in its favour. Opponents, however, argue that the demands of industry are not the only factor to be taken into account when shaping the education system of the future.

The Japanese education system has recently been attracting increased attention overseas because it is widely believed to be one of the factors that explains Japan's economic success. In particular, the high levels of achievement demonstrated by Japanese high-school students have aroused considerable admiration. In mathematics particularly, Japanese schoolchildren produce an average performance that is markedly higher than that of schoolchildren in Britain, the United States and elsewhere. For example, when a test used for 15-year-olds in Osaka prefecture was recently given to some British children of the same age, less than a third were able to beat the average Japanese mark on the test and the overall British average was well down. The superior Japanese performance was beyond dispute.

Children serving lunch at a primary school. At lunchtime the classroom is quickly converted into a canteen by the children. Primary school education coincides with an important time in a child's development and at a time when their creativity needs to be developed in order to meet the demands of their life in the future.

At the end of the day the children clean their classrooms. This happens in all schools in Japan.

The Education Department in the United States has recently completed a survey of Japanese education which identified a number of positive factors distinguishing it from the American system and enabling Japanese high-school graduates to attain the level of American university students in their second year. These included the high salaries and high prestige of the teaching profession in Japan, the much greater number of hours spent by Japanese pupils in school, and the generally disciplined and attentive environment of Japanese school classes with as many as 40 pupils in a class. Even the examination system came in for some praise on the grounds that it fostered competition and higher academic standards.

There can be little doubt that uniformity is a feature of the Japanese education system. Indeed, to the extent that the standardized national curriculum creates uniformity, it is fair to say that this is one of its goals. But the system is currently under criticism in Japan for the inhibitions it is thought to put on creative thinking and for its supposed failure to produce the innovative minds sought by industries committed to advanced technologies. Over the years, however, it has been responsible for the high level of standard literacy and numeracy; it has focussed on 'knowledge for mass production', and Japanese industry has been able to rely on this.

Pupils at High School study practical subjects such as woodwork and needlework as well as academic subjects. Competition to get into a good school is fierce and throughout the school system children face a rigorous course of exams culminating in the most important exams of all – those for entrance into university.

Hitherto, the Ministry of Education has played a central role in shaping the uniformity of Japanese primary and secondary education. The Ministry is responsible for determining the curriculum to be taught at all schools, for approving textbooks, and for regulating the standards of the private schools and universities. Its role in the future is likely to be different if uniformity ceases to be so highly regarded and to be replaced as a goal by variety and independence of mind.

University education, which was singled out for some criticism in the American report and is rarely admired by foreign observers, is another problem. Some argue that the universities only exist to give the students four undemanding years before they commit themselves to the bureaucracy or to a business corporation. The increasing competition for the declining number of plum jobs may well shift more attention to student performance at university rather than the name of the university attended.

The student radicalism of the 1960s and 1970s is a thing of the past. Demonstrations and rallies are still held by the radical factions that could then mobilize thousands of students against the Security Treaty with the United States and the Vietnam War. But now only a thin trickle of students rallies to the banners with helmets and placards, and the issues that arouse them are curiously domestic, such as university policy on student housing. As in Europe and North America, there is today less radical political activity and more conservatism at Japanese universities.

In the course of 1985 a new problem came to the fore in Japanese schools, group-bullying of other pupils and violence against the teaching staff, and this is widely seen as a symptom of educational malaise. There was a sharp rise in the number of such incidents reported in 1985 and this has been taken up by the newspapers with a considerable degree of alarm, partly because it now seems to have spread throughout the school system. 'In primary school it is bullying with words, kicking and punching. In junior high, it might be inflicting tobacco burns on the victim's arms and legs. In senior high school, it might involve putting a fire-cracker under the watch-band and lighting the fuse.'

The outbreak of serious bullying undoubtedly took educational administrators by surprise. How, then, can it be explained? Perhaps the crucial fact is that the Japanese unemployment figures have recently been creeping up. They are still way below those in Europe, North America and Australasia, but they have nevertheless tightened the competitive screw in the education system still further. In doing so it is arguable that it has increased the ranks of those whose fate is to fail in the university-competition and who therefore lose their commitment to schooling. If this is so, it offers little comfort to the government agencies trying to solve the problem.

The education system is still geared to produce people who are inured to hard work by the time they first look for a job. Now, however, the value of highly pressured work is coming under serious scrutiny. The changing population structure is making promotion prospects poorer than expected, and the potential rewards for the hard-worker are no longer so assured. Furthermore, there have been suggestions from Western countries that the hard work of the Japanese gives the country an 'unfair' advantage and is responsible for some of the trade frictions between, for example, Japan and the USA and Japan and the European Community.

Whether the Japanese do work harder than their Western counterparts is a moot point, for the dividing line between work and leisure is not always drawn in the same place. Nevertheless, it is true that the Japanese rarely take their full quota of annual paid holidays and that the five-day week is not yet standard: the banks and the Tokyo Stock Exchange are open at least two Saturday mornings a month. Furthermore, according to figures produced by the Japanese Ministry of Labour in 1986, the average number of hours worked in a year by manufacturing workers totalled 2,180: by comparison, the figure for both Britain and the USA was around 1,940.

However, not all the long hours and foregone days of leave are entirely voluntary. A British correspondent has examined the case of a salesman who works for the main Japanese telephone and telecommunications company. He was an unconventional employee in that he had taken his full entitlement of paid holidays and had resisted pressures to join in after-hours drinking and socializing. His promotion prospects have apparently been jeopardized, in spite of his good sales record, by his refusal to accept 'the Japanese idea that work suffers if we don't spend our private time together too'. There can be no doubt that others give in to the pressures if only for promotion. Nevertheless, at the same time it does seem to be true that more of the long hours are voluntary than would be credible in Western countries. For example, when the manager of a small company manufacturing shampoo offered his workforce 30 days paid holiday he met strong resistance to the idea: 'My workers got angry with me and told me that an employer who gives that much time off to his staff is irresponsible. They also told me that they are afraid that if my plan to give long holidays were to be known, our company would get a bad name.' After a struggle, he managed to persuade them to take 14 days holiday a year.

The Japanese government has recently established a body called the Leisure Development Centre, in the belief that the supposed Japanese enthusiasm for hard work is partly responsible for Japan's enormous trading surpluses. The objective is to reduce working hours and to ensure the parallel growth of leisure industries. But the Centre itself has been setting a poor example: the staff-members take even less of their annual leave entitlement than the national average and have been found working on Saturdays and Sundays preparing reports urging a shorter working week. Nevertheless, the government is undoubtedly serious in its intentions, and the Prime Minister himself has tried to set an example by taking a well-publicized long holiday and playing golf in front of television cameras for the evening news.

Golf is very popular in Japan today and was originally introduced to the country at the beginning of the century. There are over 1,000 golf courses in Japan but as space is greatly restricted and demand so great it is difficult to get a game. One solution in the overcrowded cities is the golf-driving range where golfers can practice their skills – even at night.

*Left* In a large city even tops of buildings are used to provide sporting facilities. In recent years the Japanese have become very concerned with their health and they are interested in both diet and exercise. Baseball is the most popular sport and nearly every form of modern sport is practised.

Few countries are, in fact, less suited to golf than Japan, though it remains a very popular sport. Much of the interior is mountainous and the consequent pressure of the population on the plains means that tracts of land sufficient for a golf-course are scarce and unimaginably expensive. There are nowhere near enough courses to accommodate all the would-be players – 1,200 courses for more than 10 million players – and a game on a real course is a very expensive privilege. Joining a club can be a matter of several hundred thousand pounds or dollars, and this initial fee does not cover green charges. Some of this will be paid by ones company, for as many as half the games of golf played in Japan are played with business contacts or clients. A further expense confronts the unfortunate golfer who scores a hole-in-one. Many insurance companies now provide cover specifically for this eventuality: the benefits payable amount to around £1,500, for this is the amount that the celebrations expected afterwards often cost. But there is an alternative to playing golf on a golf-course, and that is to resort to a golf practice-range, where the cost is relatively low and there is no chance of a hole-in-one. Practice-ranges are to be found in most cities, sometimes on the tops of buildings, sometimes on open plots of land. The object is to stand still and hit golf balls at the distant netting; it has the advantage of affording amounts of practice that the average Japanese golfer could never hope for on real courses and hours of exercise, and it is the Japanese solution to the problem. With floodlighting they stay open well after dusk, and can accommodate a large number in a small space.

Baseball is a sport which now has a very large following in Japan. It is also the predominant form of sporting activity in schools. There is a large number of professional teams, some of which employ American professional players on a temporary basis. But perhaps the most popular matches of all are those in the annual high school baseball competition.

*Right* A pachinko parlour. Pachinko is a simple and persistently popular game similar to pinball. Pachinko parlours are found in close proximity to most train stations and in all pleasure quarters. The game was introduced to Japan after World War II as an inexpensive form of amusement. Pachinko enthusiasts claim that the game has therapeutic value.

Another leisure activity which has taken a unique form in Japan, in response to social conditions, is the pin-ball game, or *pachinko* as it is known in Japan. Pachinko first appeared in Japan after World War II and it is now ubiquitous. Pachinko parlours, with many rows of players sitting on stools watching the small metal balls course their way down the maze of pins in front of them, announce their presence with the constant rattle. Pachinko is very big business in Japan and its popularity a puzzle. The most common explanation is that the game offers isolation in a crowd, for players rarely talk to their neighbours and for an hour or so they are alone with a machine and hundreds of ballbearings. But there are also pachinko professionals who can distinguish the machines that pay out from those that do not.

The Japanese population now stands at about 120 million. It is increasing by less than one per cent a year, and therefore the rate of population increase has declined since the war. There has been a dramatic change in the population profile of Japan which has been giving grounds for some anxiety. Today the proportion of children under the age of four has been dropping steadily while that of people aged over 65 has been increasing at an alarming rate: it is now about 10 per cent. Since the figures for Britain and Sweden are currently 14 per cent and 16 per cent respectively, there may seem to be nothing inherently alarming about this, but before the end of this century the figure is expected to have risen to 20 per cent or even more, which will probably then be the highest percentage in the world. For more than a century the proportion of people aged over 65 had been steady at a figure of between five and seven per cent.

The reasons for these changes are not far to seek. The rising standard of medical care combined with a predominantly fat-free diet has resulted in the highest life-expectancy figures in the world for both men and

These senior citizens queue for a show of 'enka' singing. Enka are both traditional and popular songs which appeal to a wide audience. Of Japan's population of 120 million some 10 per cent is aged over 65 and by the end of the century this is expected to rise to 20 per cent – the highest percentage in the world.

women. For men it is around 79 and for women 83, whereas 40 years ago Japanese had a life expectancy of just over 50 years. Fewer babies are being born today and the size of an average family has declined drasticaly since the 1930s. Japan's medical and welfare services will have to find ways of coping with the increased burden of its elderly population. There will also be increasing financial pressures and a further strain on what is already a very tight housing market.

How these problems will be met remains to be seen. The only concrete proposal put forward has a touch of the bizarre about it: the Japanese Ministry of International Trade and Industry has been carefully considering the idea of setting up retirement villages overseas. The advantageous exchange rate for the yen would enable the residents to live comfortably on their Japanese pensions. A survey found that Australia and Canada were the most favoured destinations for people of retiring age, and the Ministry has proposed to the Australian government that the first batches of Japanese arrive in 1992. There has been opposition to this plan from the Returned Servicemen's League, one of whose representatives has said that: 'These ageing Japanese who would be coming here would be the very people we were fighting against.' On the other hand, Japan is now Australia's biggest trading partner and the source of a growing number of tourists. But any attractions that the scheme might have in terms of a substantial investment in yen will have to be weighed against the extra burden that would be imposed on Australia's own health and welfare services.

It is difficult to imagine that this scheme could be anything other than an interim solution for a small minority of the retired population. For them the attractions will have to be weighed against the prospect of being almost entirely cut off from their families in Japan. Even though the scheme has the support of some old people's associations and some companies that are concerned for the retirement prospects of their employees, those who do choose to take it up will face some real problems. As one man coming up to retirement told a foreign journalist, 'Local food and customs will take a lot of getting used to. It's not easy at 65 to fit into a new cultural environment. They just want to get rid of us.'

What might persuade the reluctant to opt for a new life overseas is the financial argument. The subsidy for medical benefits for those over 70 is due to be reduced considerably and the pension benefits provided by the state have to be supplemented by their savings accumulated over their working lives. Since the traditional extended-family pattern has begun to disintegrate, it is clear that an increasing number of retired couples in Japan will have to budget for the expense of living alone. For reasons of this sort, then, living in a retirement village abroad could hold some attractions – so long, of course, as the yen continues to rise in the world currency markets.

What remains very uncertain is whether the scheme will appeal to any of the countries that are currently being considered by the Japanese government. The position of the elderly in Japan today has been much affected by the enormous changes that have taken place in Japanese domestic life since the war, and the probability is that solutions will have to be found which are not dependent on the goodwill of other countries.

## CHAPTER SEVEN

# International Society and Japan

*Left* A priest dances a traditional dance at a Shinto shrine at Miyajima. During the dance he wards off evil spirits.

*Below* Sumo wrestlers preparing a meal. Sumo wrestling is a highly professional sport and the oldest in Japan. Most wrestlers weigh between 250 and 350 pounds. The outcome of the fight is decided when any part of the body, except the feet, touches the ground or when the wrestler leaves the ring.

Some years ago *sushi* (rice and raw fish) and other Japanese dishes were as unknown as the kabuki theatre and sumo wrestling. Now, however, there are sushi restaurants in London, New York, Toronto, Sydney and Paris. Kabuki troupes have visited Europe and North America, and Westerners have performed in kabuki plays, such as those staged by the Canadian Academy in Kobe. Sumo tournaments have been held in Paris and sumo wrestlers have been used to promote various products in the United States, including Diet Coke; and several Hawaiians have made successful careers for themselves as sumo wrestlers in Japan. To this extent, then, Japanese culture is acquiring an international flavour. But is that all there is to 'international understanding'?

It has taken a long time for Western nations and Asian neighbours alike to grasp the implications of Japan's rapid economic growth. It is now not only possible that Japan might soon become the richest country in the world but it is being widely predicted that this will in fact happen by the end of the decade. Whether this prediction is fulfilled on time or not, there

can be little doubt that the Japanese share of world business is still on the increase, and at the inevitable expense of those countries used to considering themselves the richest.

Signs that this is happening have already appeared in banking. In 1984 the Japanese share of the international banking market was 23 per cent, while the United States' share was 26 per cent and the British 8 per cent. By September 1986, just two years later, the Japanese share had risen to 31 per cent while the American and British shares had fallen to 18 per cent and 6 per cent respectively. To some extent it is the rise of the yen and the fall of the dollar that have been responsible for the advance of the Japanese banks

A piper from the internationally famous Kodo Ensemble practicing in the woods. The Kodo group of dancers and musicians has toured Europe and America on several occasions to wide acclaim.

176

on the world market, but, in the words of a recent report, the 'general dynamism and competitiveness' of the Japanese banks in their international operations have been as important a factor here as they were earlier in the growth of Japanese manufacturing industries.

The expansion of the Japanese economy in world markets is not only a matter of the sale and distribution of Japanese goods and services. It is also, to an increasing extent, a matter of the establishment of subsidiaries and sister companies overseas, like the new Nissan plant in the north of England, and even of the purchase of foreign companies, such as the acquisition by two Japanese companies in 1986 of Tomatin Distillers, a distiller

One of the Kodo drummers during a spectacular outdoor performance of the Ensemble

of Scotch whisky. These moves are a product partly of the fear of protectionism, which could restrict the export of goods made in Japan, and partly of the search for cheaper labour overseas. As a result, Japan has become a more active participant in international society than before and has undergone a degree of 'internationalization' – a word popularized by Prime Minister Nakasone. Japanese are living and working abroad in growing numbers, and the same is true of foreigners resident in Japan, but there have been some problems experienced by both groups which suggest that 'internationalization' may take some time to achieve.

The establishment of plants overseas necessitates moving managerial personnel abroad in order to oversee operations. NEC, for example, the huge Japanese computer and communications company, has now about 500 Japanese managers at its plants in America and elsewhere, and has established its own Institute for International Studies to prepare prospective managers and their families for life abroad. The preparation ranges from Western table-manners to intensive language training programmes in which participants are fined every time they use Japanese. An important part of the programme is the mock-bargaining sessions which train managers how to negotiate with their distributors or with trade unions in English. All this is very different from the 1970s, when trial and error was the only method of Japanese managers working overseas and very different too from the practice of British or American firms operating in Japan: how many of them give their expatriate managers training in Japanese, let alone teach them how to negotiate in Japanese?

For expatriates everywhere, life abroad is a mixture of the frustrations and stimulations of a different environment, and it is not always easy to fit back into life at home again. This is as true of Japanese as it is of Britains, Americans and Australians, but there is an added difficulty in Japan caused by very different working practices at home and abroad, even when employed by the same company. In some cases patterns of family life have to change as a result. One woman interviewed by the *Wall Street Journal*'s correspondent found the increased demands on her husband's time when they returned to Japan after 13 years abroad hard to bear: 'In the US we would have people to our home during the week. I talked to my husband and understood his job. In Japan there are weeks when there isn't a single weekday that I can have dinner with my husband – weekends only.' Difficulties of this sort are well recognized now and some of the major Japanese companies have set up counselling programmes for returning employees.

One of the most persistent worries affecting Japanese given overseas assignments is the education of their children. The brave send their children to local schools to give them a more international upbringing than they could have in Japan and a chance of learning another language. There is the risk, however, that a child may have severe difficulties fitting into the Japanese education system again after several years abroad. There are ways around this problem, such as the use of Japanese educational materials to ensure that children do not fall behind their peers in their knowledge of the Japanese written language. There are also private schools and universities in Japan which operate partly in English to cater to the foreign population

Members of the Kodo Ensemble relax in their simple quarters. The room is spacious and uncluttered, with tatami mats covering the floor. Shoes are not worn inside as is the Japanese custom – bare feet or socks on the mats and slippers on wooden floors are the general rule.

and which are now admitting Japanese who have been educated abroad. It seems to be true that the major companies are still reluctant to recruit graduates with this sort of educational experience, though there are enhanced opportunities to work for one of the growing numbers of foreign companies now operating in Japan.

Some who have been educated abroad choose not to return to Japan. Kazuo Ishiguro was born in Japan but came to England as a boy in 1960 with his parents and after being educated in England chose to stay. He recently won a major British literary prize for his novel, *An Artist of the Floating World*, which he wrote in English. Asked why he had not returned to Japan, he had something rather caustic to say:

> The Japanese are very racist. They're very peculiar about foreigners. They'll treat certain foreigners as guests, politely, at a distance, in a very hospitable way, and they'll expect you to do everything wrong and behave in an improper manner. If I go there they'll think: here's a Japanese, he doesn't speak Japanese in the correct way, he doesn't address people in the correct language, he does everything wrong. And they'll generally be rather unsympathetic anyway to the idea of a Japanese who went abroad. Japanese who stay away from home too long have always been regarded as rather contaminated. Someone who is completely Westernized as I am has very few excuses in Japan. They'll think I'm some kind of uncivilized moron.

All expatriates suffer this fate to some extent, but it is precisely to avoid excluding their children irretrievably from Japanese society that some parents choose to leave their families behind in Japan or to send their children to one of the Japanese schools abroad. These have been growing in number in recent years and there has been pressure on the Ministry of Education to make regular Japanese education available to more children living abroad. That is undoubtedly the best way to ensure that children will not be placed at a disadvantage in the competition for university places and good jobs should they return to Japan, but equally surely it is a step that will reduce the pace of internationalization.

How, on the other hand, do foreign residents fare in Japan? It will certainly be many years before a Briton manages to emulate the achievement of Kazuo Ishiguro. This is not so much for linguistic reasons, for there are now many young non-Japanese brought up to Japan who speak flawless Japanese. It is simply that he or she will not be able to obtain a Japanese passport, to vote, or otherwise to assume the role in Japanese society that Kazuo Ishiguro has assumed in Britain. Until recently, when the law was relaxed slightly, it has been very difficult to win permanent residence status, and all but impossible to acquire Japanese nationality, even for foreigners married to Japanese. This applied equally to members of the Korean minority in Japan, a minority of around 700,000 most of whom are the decendants of Korean labourers conscripted to work in Japan during World War II: their families have now lived in Japan for several generations, they speak Japanese, and they are Japanese in all but nationality. The Immigration Department has consistently confused questions of nationality with questions of ethnic origin, such that long-time residents married to Japanese remain aliens while Americans of even distant Japanese decent, for example, have much less difficulty gaining Japanese nationality.

While the immigration and nationality laws are only being revised at a painfully slow pace, there have been more signs of a willingness to open the job market in Japan to non-Japanese. There have always been openings for foreigners to teach their native languages in Japan, or work as interpreters or translators, but teaching other subjects, particularly in the national universities, was out of the question until 1982 when the law was changed. Today there are scientific teachers of various nationalities, including

Inside the Shinto Itsukushima Shrine at Miyajima. This is one of the greatest shrines in Japan and is also one of the three most famous sights in the country. The shrine was founded in the sixth century and enlarged in later centuries.

Japanese-Koreans, working in the national universities. Similarly, several banks and other companies have begun, albeit still on a small scale, to appoint non-Japanese personnel to career positions. Most of the Americans, Australians, Koreans and others who have taken such positions already have a good grasp of the language.

There is some unease in Japan about the process of internationalization. Kazuo Ishiguro described the Japanese as 'racialist', while Kase Hideaki, a conservative Japanese writer resident in Japan, has put it more simply, 'Japanese are very tribal'. Kase is the son of a former Japanese ambassador to the United Nations, but in spite of his background he expressed undisguised relief when Prince Hiro, the emperor's eldest grandson, came to the end of his two years of postgraduate study at Oxford and returned to Japan. 'Everybody was worried that Prince Hiro would marry a foreigner. That would be a real national crisis. Personally, I would find it revolting.' Royal marriages are of little more than symbolic importance, however, and the unease about internationalization is rooted instead in the self-contained and secluded nature of much of Japanese history. Japan has neither the close international contacts common in Europe nor the mix of nationalities of North America or Australia. And even today there are still fewer foreign faces in Japanese cities than in Paris, London or New York, for example. In such circumstances, therefore, it is perhaps not surprising if part of the population continues to feel uncomfortable about the idea of internationalization.

As a result there is a feeling that it is safer for Japan to play a less prominent international role, perhaps for fear of becoming embroiled in disputes or of jeopardizing export markets. It is very difficult, however, to see how a country with a major stake in the economic activity of the world can continue to remain aloof from it. Foreign affairs are rarely an important

A Japanese fashion show. As Japan's culture acquires an international flavour so too does its fashion. Western designers are popular while in the West several Japanese designers have become famous in recent years with showrooms in the capital cities of several countries.

*Above left* Japanese sandals for sale. These are often worn in the warm, humid summers and generally around one's neighbourhood and are said to be healthy for the feet as the big toe is separated from the other toes.

*Above right* The Japanese enjoy a variety of dried and semi-dried fish. In the days before refrigeration and high-speed transportation, drying was the only way to preserve fish so that it could be transported out of season. Here a fisherman's wife sprinkles sesame seeds on some freshly caught fish before they are dried. Dried fish is still the favourite snack to accompany beer or sake.

consideration in Japanese politics, and recent events have shown this can have consequences that are diplomatically embarrassing and also economically damaging. The attempts, for example, by the Ministry of Education to alter the sections in school textbooks dealing with the Rape of Nanking and the occupation of Korea resulted in boycotts of Japanese goods and anti-Japanese demonstrations in Peking and Seoul. When Prime Minister Nakasone made his official visit to the Yasukuni shrine, to pay tribute to the souls of those who have died in war, there were further anti-Japanese demonstrations in China and charges of revived Japanese militarism. There may well be political factors at work behind the demonstrations, in view of the substantial trade surplus Japan enjoys with China and the desire of the Chinese government for more Japanese investment and technology. Nevertheless, the Japanese government seems to have underestimated Chinese sensitivity on this score and to have placed itself in a position of choosing between offending a major foreign market or the bulk of the ruling Liberal-Democratic Party.

The importance of foreign-policy issues has also been underlined by the ever-increasing trade surpluses Japan now enjoys with most of its trading partners. Protectionist sentiment has been growing in the legislative assemblies and trade unions of the United States, the European Community,

Canada, Australasia, and elsewhere. It is partly as a result of this trend that a consensus of opinion has begun to emerge in Japan on the need to integrate the country into world affairs more closely and to stimulate domestic growth so as to reduce Japan's dependence on export earnings.

At a news conference at the end of 1985 the Prime Minister expressed a radically new understanding of the relationship between foreign policy and economic policy in so far as Japan is concerned:

> Japan's social and economic structure has been oriented towards exports – it had to be for our postwar reconstruction. But we must ask ourselves: can Japan go on living with current account surpluses of 40 or 50 billion dollars a year? It's like winning every time you play a game of mah-jong. In the end no one will play with you.

The rise in the value of the yen may reduce the trade surpluses, but there is little sign of that happening yet. The prices of imported goods have dropped only marginally, while Japanese export prices have yet to rise as significantly as the changing exchange rate would lead one to expect. The main results so far have been a rapid rise in the number of bankruptcies among small companies unable to absorb losses like the large companies; signs that the unemployment rate is rising; a tendency to shift manufacturing industry overseas to take advantage of lower wages; and a widespread feeling in Japan that the economy is in difficulties. But the trade surpluses are continuing to grow and there is increasing danger that protectionist sentiments will be translated into action and several countries will stop playing mah-jong with Japan.

Why have the trade imbalances become so large in the first place? Peter Drucker, a prominent American writer on economic affairs, has one explanation:

Sorting the catch at Nagasaki fish market. Nagasaki is one of Japan's oldest and busiest ports. Japan is a major fishing nation with coastal fishing, deep-sea trawling and fish farming carried out.

'Why is the West obsessed with our exports?' every Japanese visitor asks. 'The West Germans export even more and their trade surpluses are also growing rapidly.' But there is a difference – though the Japanese are oblivious to it. The West Germans do indeed top the Japanese as exporters of manufactured goods – only the US exports more. But the West Germans are also the world's second-largest importers of such goods – again topped only by the US. The Japanese, however, only sell; they do not buy. They practice adversarial trade.

The Japanese assert that it is not their fault that we find their goods more attractive than what we produce ourselves, and say that their export strength is simply the result of their working harder and doing a better job, whether in design, in quality, in price or in service. This is right on the whole – Japan Inc. is largely a figment of the Western imagination. But it is also irrelevant. Adversarial trade will not be tolerated very long.

Drucker is prepared to accept, then, that it is their quality which has created the demand for Japanese goods, but argues that trade imbalances arise because the Japanese will not buy Western goods. Yet if Japanese goods really are superior as he allows, then there is little reason to be surprised if Japanese consumers prefer local products.

It is a fact that Japan buys less than it sells. Some assert that this is because it will not buy as a matter of policy and has erected barriers to prevent imports, or that Japanese consumers are averse to buying foreign goods for patriotic reasons; others argue that the sellers have not made sufficient effort to tune their products and sales techniques to the Japanese market. So where does the truth lie?

On the one hand, Mr Nakasone's Action Programme to open up the domestic market to imports from abroad is a tacit admission that there have been barriers hitherto:

It is a blueprint for what is probably the most sweeping reform of economic and trade practices, as well as social attitudes and behaviour, ever proposed for a modern industrial society. It sets out cuts in tariffs in manufactured goods that will give Japan the most liberal tariff regime in the world. It specifies more than 250 changes in laws and regulations to bring Japan's system of industrial standards and its import procedures into line with those in the West. It promises active steps to get private firms and government agencies to import more from abroad.

But even before this Action Programme was announced the Organization for Economic Cooperation and Development had found in its survey of Japan that the average tariff rates were lower than those in Europe and America. Similarly, it found that Japan imposed fewer quotas on imports, with the exception of the agricultural sector: here the traditional reliance of the Liberal-Democratic Party on the rural vote is undoubtedly the major factor. Some products, it is pointed out, are still excluded from the reforms, such as oranges and other agricultural products, chocolates, cosmetics and pharmaceutical products. Nevertheless, the judgment of observers without a brief for the Japanese government is that tariffs and quotas are not keeping imports out of Japan.

It is also commonly argued that the complex Japanese scheme for the distribution of goods acts as an invisible, or 'non-tariff', barrier to imported

The middlemen at work auctioning the morning's catch at Tsukiji Fish Market. There is a fantastic range of fresh fish in Japan much of which may be unfamiliar to Westerners.

goods. 'Why does Japan, a country that so prides itself on efficiency and the most up-to-date technology, allow such a convoluted and archaic distribution system to continue to exist in the first place?' The system *is* convoluted, for goods pass through the hands of many more middlemen than is usual in Western countries. For instance, in Toyko's famous fish market a freshly landed tuna may pass through four different middlemen within a few hours. Still more people will be involved in the subsequent process of getting the fish to the stomach of the consumer. The system does, however, serve two functions in Japan: one is the social one of providing greater employment and the other is the practical one of ensuring a constant supply of goods without having to store them on the premises weeks before they are sold. The distribution system is an inconvenience for foreign importers, but it is inconvenient for new Japanese companies trying to break into the market too. A survey of foreign executives in Japan carried out in 1983 found that only 28 per cent thought that national business practices should be respected while over 60 per cent considered that they should be changed to suit foreign companies. Would they be willing to see business practices in their own countries changed to suit Japanese, or Korean, or Taiwanese companies?

On the other hand, how much effort have the sellers made? There are enough examples to show that it is clearly not impossible for foreign imports to be successful in Japan.

Americans who travel to Japan are often confused by what they see. At home they hear many a complaint about impenetrable Japanese markets, but in Japan they're deluged by American logos and trademarks: Baskin-Robbins, Coca-Cola, Schick, Kodak, Tupperware. Clearly, many American companies are doing well in Japan, and some are even outdoing Japanese rivals on their own turf.

This is undoubtedly true. The soft-drink market is dominated by Coca-Cola, instant coffee by Nestlé, Indian teas by Twinings, electric shavers by Braun, and so on. British duffle coats have been selling well in Japan recently, so too have fashion accessories like scarves and shawls. There is no evidence here of an aversion in Japan to imported products as such.

For every success story there are several failures. An American company, for example, became the first ever to sell personal computers in Japan. Its products, however, did not sell because they could not process written Japanese and the instruction manuals were in English. Trade barriers are not at work here: it is simply a matter of crass marketing. If the Japanese computer-printers that are now selling well in Europe and America could only print in Japanese and came with Japanese instruction manuals, who would buy them? Poor marketing and the blithe assumption that business in Japan is conducted much the same as at home cause many failures.

There can be no doubt that exporting to Japan is a frustrating and difficult experience for Western companies. The language is unfamiliar, and so too are patterns of entertainment, customs and manners. Business is conducted and decisions reached in ways that often puzzle an ill-prepared foreign executive, and years of business experience elsewhere seem to be of no use at all. But Japan's population is 120 million, and for such a market it is worth persevering. This is a point put strongly by the Australian Trade Mission to Japan in 1984:

> The Japanese market for manufactures and services is open for the right produce, correctly and energetically marketed. To the Japanese, quality is a total concept and applies not only to stringent production standards but to the whole of the company's activities encompassing marketing, sales, administration and service. To succeed in Japan, Australian companies must be able to match the standards the Japanese have set for themselves. Australian suppliers hoping to succeed in the Japanese market must be prepared to alter product design and packaging to suit market requirements.

Japanese consumers demand unusually high levels of quality and service. Some British cars as a result have to be stripped down and reassembled in Japan because of poor quality controls during the manufacturing process in Britain. Similarly, gift boxes have to be designed for many foreign imports before they can attract purchasers in Japan. Perhaps the Japanese consumer is excessively demanding, or perhaps British and American consumers are too tolerant of poor quality, but whichever the case the expectations of Japanese consumers have to be met by foreign and Japanese firms alike. Exporters remain ignorant of the particular characteristics of the Japanese market at their peril. A British executive who had worked for a Japanese company in Britain recently established a company to help British firms in the Japanese market and developed an introductory course on Japan aimed at businessmen and women. The course covered business practices in Japan, domestic, social and historical factors affecting the Japanese market, but only a tiny handful of companies felt that they needed this information, let alone knowledge of the language.

Although the idea that the industrialized West should begin to learn from Japan's success is gaining more support today, there remains much

Shinto priests bow at the Tzumo Taisha shrine. Bowing is a mark of respect and is used both when greeting people and when taking one's leave.

about Japan that many Britons and Americans find unattractive. The following extracts illustrate the differing attitudes very neatly. Akira, the Japanese academic who figures in David Lodge's comic novel *Small World* lives in a minute flat:

> He cannot actually stand up in it, and on unlocking the door, and having taken off his shoes, is obliged to crawl, rather than step, inside. The apartment, or living unit, is like a very luxurious padded cell. . . . Four hundred identical cells are stacked and interlocked in this building, like a tower of eggboxes.

But Akira sees this flat with very different eyes:

> How much time people waste in walking from one room to another – especially in the West! Space is time. Akira was particularly shocked by the waste of both in Californian homes he visited during his graduate studies in the United States: separate rooms not just for sleeping, eating and excreting, but also for cooking, studying, entertaining, watching television, playing games, washing clothes and practising hobbies – all spread out profligately over acres of land, so that it could take a whole minute to walk from say, one's bedroom to one's study.

Akira's views have been exaggerated for comic effect, but this example will nevertheless serve to show that here are two sides to questions that often seem cut and dried to Britons and Americans. Japan is beginning to challenge values that have been taken for granted in the West and to be critical of weaknesses where Japan is felt to have strengths. In the ferment of ideas that is beginning to determine the shape of the twenty-first century, the contribution of Japan is impossible to ignore. Perhaps the most important lesson that the world can learn from Japan is that the West can no longer claim to oversee the development of the planet.

# Bibliographical References

The references have been set out chapter by chapter. The number set in **bold** refers to the page in the narrative and the first words of each quote are given.

## CHAPTER ONE

**9** 'messenger from the black hole': T. Umesao, ed., *Seventy-seven Keys to the Civilization of Japan* (The Plaza Hotel, Osaka, 1983), p.iii.

**13** 'Judging by': M. Cooper, *They Came to Japan: An Anthology of European Reports on Japan, 1543-1640* (University of California Press, Berkeley, 1965), p.60.

**14** 'It is remarkable': *ibid* p.63

**14** 'I saw one': Cooper, *They Came to Japan*, p.156 (spelling modernized).

**15** 'The city': Cooper, *They Came to Japan*, p.277.

**15** 'Although they copy': *ibid* p.254.

**15** 'Their first': Cooper, *ibid* p.46.

**17** 'English art': J-P. Lehmann, *The Image of Japan: From Feudal Isolation to World Power, 1850-1905* (George Allen and Unwin, London, 1978), p.57.

**17** 'Japanese cleanliness': *ibid* p.46.

**18** 'The Japanese': *ibid* p.51.

**25** 'No longer': *Far Eastern Economic Review* 28 (March 1985), p.43.

## CHAPTER TWO

**44** 'I saw': Cooper, *They Came to Japan*, p.388 (spelling modernized).

**44** 'A European': G. K. Goodman, *Japan: The Dutch Experience* (The Athlone Press, London, 1986), pp.21-2.

**44** 'How then': *ibid* p.22.

**54** 'Men and women': M. Miyoshi, *As We Saw Them* (University of California Press, Berkeley, 1965), p.71.

## CHAPTER THREE

**65** 'I intend': Adriana Boscaro, *101 Letters of Hideyoshi* (Sophia University, Tokyo, 1975), p.53.

**66** 'I repeat': *ibid* p.77.

**71** 'the Japanese navy': *The War in the Far East, 1904-1905, by the Military Correspondent of The Times* (London, 1905).

**71** 'We were': A. Novikoff-Priboy, *Tsushima*, translated by E. & C. Paul (George Allen and Unwin, London, 1936), pp.167, 175 and 180.

**76** 'It is inevitable': Tota Ishimaru, *Japan Must Fight Britain* (London, 1936), p.xi.

**76** 'The report': *ibid* p.241-2.

**78** 'Those Japs': quoted in J. W. Dower, *War Without Mercy* (Faber & Faber, London, 1986), p.101.

**78** 'I hope': Mary Thomas, *In the Shadow of the Rising Sun* (Maruzen Asia, Singapore, 1983, p.80.

**78** 'looks like': Leocadio de Asis, *From Bataan to Tokyo: Diary of a Filipino Student in Wartime Japan* (Center for East Asia Studies, University of Kansas, 1979), p.139.

**79** 'how funny': quoted in Ben-Ami Shillomy, *Politics and Culture in Wartime Japan* (Clarendon Press, Oxford, 1981), p.144.

**82** 'We shot': quoted in J. W. Dower, *War Without Mercy* (Faber & Faber, London, 1986), p.64.

**82** 'It was freely': ibid. p.70.

## CHAPTER FOUR

**99** 'Our hosts': *The Autobiography of Yukichi Fukuzawa*, translated by E. Kiyooka (Columbia University Press, New York, 1966), p.115.

**99** 'Coming directly': quoted in H. J. Jones, *Live Machines: Hired Foreigners and Meiji Japan* (Paul Norbury Publications, Tenterden, Kent, 1980), p.73.

**104** 'The care': Joseph d'Autremer, *The Japanese Empire and its Economic Conditions* (T. Fisher Unwin, London, 1910), p.238.

**106** 'One of the most': N. Garnett, 'Clues to an innovation paradox', *Financial Times*, 9 May 1986.

## CHAPTER FIVE

**111** 'in function': T. Umesao, ed., *Seventy-seven Keys to the Civilization of Japan* (The Plaza Hotel, Osaka, 1983), p.188.

**112** 'the price': Robert Whymant, 'The friendly neighbourhood police state', *The Guardian*, 5 September 1975.

**112** 'O we': Walter L. Ames, *Police and Community in Japan* (University of California Press, Berkeley, 1981), p.178.

**114** 'A woman': Robert Whymant, 'The friendly neighbourhood police state', *The Guardian*, 5 September 1975.

**115** 'when I visited': Walter L. Ames, *Police and Community in Japan* (University of California Press, Berkeley, 1981), p.114.

**121** 'The yakuza': Philippe Pons, 'Yamaguchigumi – the Japanese mafia', *The Guardian Weekly*, 13 May 1979, p.16.

**126** 'To pray for': Irara Saikaku, *The Life of an Amorous Woman* translated by Ivan Morris (New Directions, New York, 1969), pp.203-4. Copyright © 1963 by UNESCO.

**130** 'It is impossible': Rutherford Alcock, *The Capital of the Tycoon* (Longman, Green, Longman, Roberts & Green, London, 1863), pp.122-3.

**131** 'We all now realized': quoted in Ty & Kiyoko Heineken, *Tansu: Traditional Japanese Cabinetry* (Weatherhill, Tokyo, 1981), pp.22-3.

**135** 'The lack of what': Ronald Dore, *Shinohata: A Portrait of a Japanese Village* (Allen Lane, London, 1978), p.283.

**138** 'In 1984': *The New Scientist*, 21 March 1985, p.41.

**141** 'the lowest of all': quoted in George DeVos and Hiroshi Wagatsuma, eds, *Japan's Invisible Race: Caste in Culture and Personality* (University of California Press, Berkeley, 1966), p.38.

**141** 'You will feel': *The Broken Commandment*, by Shimazaki Toson, translated by Kenneth Strong (University of Tokyo Press, 1974), pp.229-30. Copyright © 1974 by UNESCO.

## CHAPTER SIX

**155** 'She is not often': quoted in Christine Chapman, 'Century-Old Letters From a Japanese Pioneer', *International Herald Tribune*, 2 July 1986.

**156** 'Upon this occasion': Alice Mabel Bacon, *A Japanese Intrerior* (Gay and Bird, London, 1893).

**156** 'The alternative': Alice Mabel Bacon, *Japanese Girls and Women* (Gay and Bird, London, 1891), p.57.

**157** 'arranged marriages': quoted in Robert O. Blood, *Love Match and Arranged Marriage*, (The Free Press, New York, 1967). p.6.

**157** 'marriage partners': quoted in Gail Bernstein, 'Women in Rural Japan', in J. Lebra, et el., *Women in Changing Japan* (Westview Press, Boulder, 1976), p.46.

**158** 'Japanese public': Alice Mabel Bacon, *Japanese Girls and Women* (Gay and Bird, London, 1891), p.290-1.

**160** 'There seems no doubt': *ibid* p.260.

**160** 'holds and exercises': Takie Sugiyama Lebra, *Japanese Women: Constraint and Fulfilment* (University of Hawaii Press, Honolulu, 1984), p.ix.

**163** 'urging my sex': Baroness Shidzue Ishimoto, *Facing Two Ways: The Story of My Life* (Farrar & Rinehart, New York, 1935), p.232.

**166** 'knowledge for mass production': Andrew Horvat, 'Knowledge for mass production', *The Independent*, 5 February 1987.

**168** 'In primary school': B. Wysocki, 'Asian Bullies', *The Wall Street Journal*, 12 November 1985. © Dow Jones & Company Inc. 1985. All Rights Reserved.

**168** 'the Japanese idea': Robert Whymant, 'Stirrings of revolt over the company man ethos'. *The Guardian*, 24 January 1986.

**169** 'My workers': quoted in Andrew Horvat, 'Yen for work thwarts Tokyo', *The Independent*, 17 December 1987.

**173** 'These ageing Japanese': *The Independent*, 5 February 1987.

**173** 'Local food': Philippe Pons, 'Bleak prospects face Japan's ageing population', *The Guardian Weekly*, 8 February 1987.

## CHAPTER SEVEN

**178** 'In the US': E. S. Browning, 'Unhappy Returns', *The Wall Street Journal*, 6 May 1986. © Dow Jones & Company Inc. 1986. All Rights Reserved.

**179** 'The Japanese are': *The Literary Review* (January 1987), p.19.

**181** 'Everybody was worried': Bernard Wysocki, 'Closed Society', *The Wall Street Journal*, 13 November 1986. © Dow Jones & Company Inc. 1986. All Rights Reserved.

**183** 'Japan's social and economic': quoted in William Horsley, 'Losing at mah-jong', *The Listener*, 12 December 1985, p.9.

**184** 'Why is the West': Peter F. Drucker, 'Japan and Adversarial Trade', *The Wall Street Journal*, 1 April 1986.

**184** 'It is a blueprint': William Horsley, 'Losing at mah-jong', *The Listener*, 12 December 1905, p.9.

**185** 'Why does Japan': Laurence Bresler, 'You Won't Find a Bargain in Tokyo', *The Wall Street Journal*, 20 October 1986.

**185** 'Americans who travel': Peter Grilli, 'In Favor of the Long View', *The Wall Street Journal*, 13 November 1986.

**186** 'The Japanese market': Australian Department of Trade, *Report of the High-Level Trade Mission to Japan* (Australian Government Publishing Service, Canberra, 1984), p.5.

**187** 'He cannot actually': David Lodge, *Small World* (Penguin Books, Harmondsworth, 1985.), p.103. Copyright © Secker & Warburg.

**187** 'How much time': *ibid* p.103.

# Index

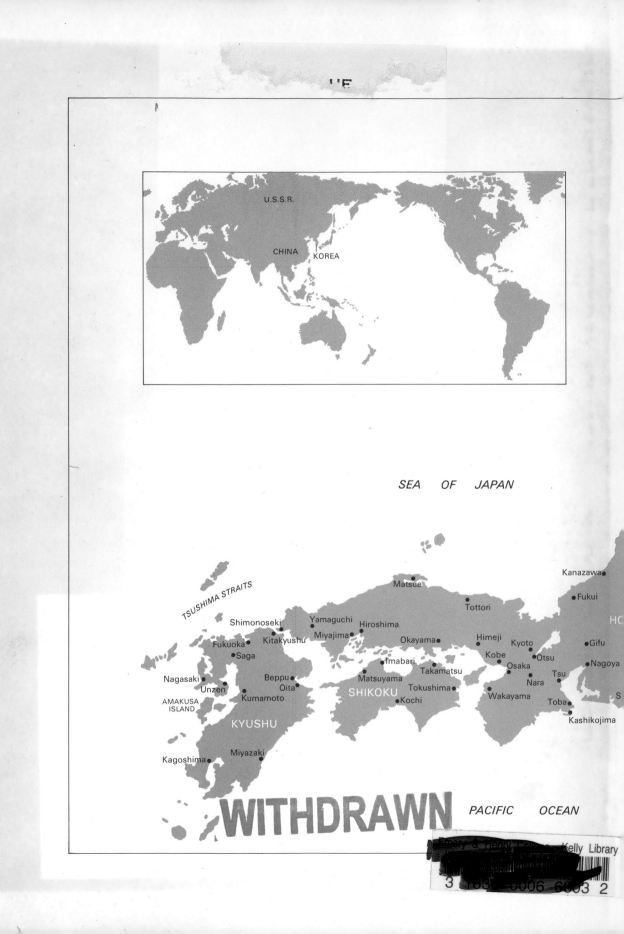

U.S.S.R.

CHINA

KOREA

SEA OF JAPAN

Kanazawa

Fukui

Matsue

Tottori

TSUSHIMA STRAITS

Shimonoseki

Yamaguchi

Hiroshima

HC

Miyajima

Okayama

Himeji

Kyoto

Gifu

Fukuoka

Kitakyushu

Kobe

Otsu

Saga

Osaka

Nagoya

Imabari

Tsu

Nagasaki

Beppu

Matsuyama

Takamatsu

Nara

Unzen

Oita

Tokushima

Wakayama

AMAKUSA
ISLAND

Kumamoto

SHIKOKU

Toba

S

Kochi

Kashikojima

KYUSHU

Kagoshima

Miyazaki

PACIFIC OCEAN